I WILL
ALWAYS
OVERCOME

SHANE WINNINGS

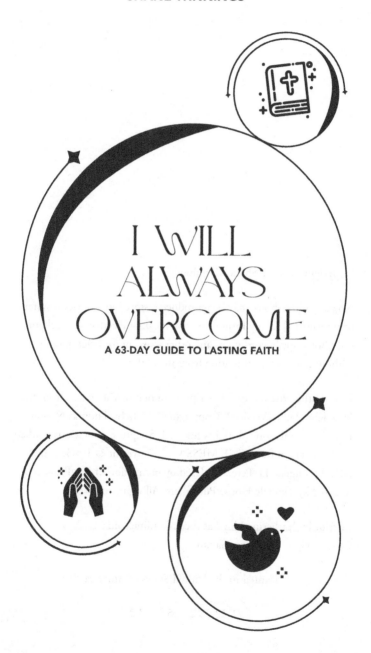

I WILL ALWAYS ALWAYS OVERCOME

A 63-DAY GUIDE TO LASTING FAITH

CONTENTS

Introduction 1

WEEKS 1–3: IDENTITY

*Establishing biblical truths about who God is
and who you are in Him.*

Day 1 – I Am Made in God's Image 7

Day 2 – I Am Loved by God 9

Day 3 – I Am Who God Says I Am 11

Day 4 – God Desires Me 13

Day 5 – I Am Found 15

Day 6 – I Am His Joy 17

Day 7 – I Am Forgiven, Not Condemned 19

Day 8 – I Am a New Creation 21

Day 9 – I Am Free from Sin 23

Day 10 – I Am a Saint, Not a Sinner 26

Day 11 – I Am Not a Mistake 28

Day 12 – My Life Has Purpose 30

Day 13 – I Live by the Spirit 32

Day 14 – I Am Not My Circumstances 34

Day 15 – No One Owes Me Anything 36

Day 16 – I Am Not Alone 38

Day 17 – I Was Made to Shine 40

Day 18 – I Am Qualified by Him 43

Day 19 – I Was Made to Love 46

Day 20 – I Have Something to Give 49

Day 21 – I Am Not Afraid 51

WEEKS 4–6: AUTHORITY

*Understanding the authority we have in Christ
and dismantling the lies that come against it.*

Day 22 – I Have the Same Spirit as Jesus Did. 57

Day 23 – God Wants to Use Me 60

Day 24 – I Can Hear God 63

Day 25 – God Can Hear Me 66

Day 26 – Darkness Flees When I Have Faith. 69

Day 27 – I Can Move God's Heart. 72

Day 28 – Spiritual Gifts Are for Me 75

Day 29 – I Can Move Mountains 78

Day 30 – I Can Heal the Sick. 81

Day 31 – I Can Cast Out Demons 84

Day 32 – I Can Raise the Dead. 87

Day 33 – I Can Preach the Gospel. 90

Day 34 – I Can Prophesy 93

Day 35 – I Can Forgive. 96

Day 36 – I Can Overcome Temptation .99

Day 37 – I Can Break Off Curses 102

Day 38 – I Can Tear Down Lies. 105

Day 39 – I Can Change My Nation 108

Day 40 – I Can Make Disciples. 111

Day 41 – My Intercession Is Warfare 114

Day 42 – I Can Overcome the Enemy. .117

WEEKS 7–9: ACTIVATION

*Declaring the truth of your purpose and destiny in Christ,
and dismantling fear of the unknown.*

Day 43 – I Will Be a Doer of the Word 123

Day 44 – I Will Lay Hands on the Sick. .126

Day 45 – I Will Be Generous. 129

Day 46 – I Will Pray for Those in Need. 132

Day 47 – I Will Take Risks 135

Day 48 – I Will Surrender to God 138

Day 49 – I Will Tell Someone About Jesus. 141

Day 50 – I Will Fast. 144

Day 51 – I Will Make Time for God. 147

Day 52 – I Will Face and Overcome My Fears 150

Day 53 – I Will Get Connected. 153

Day 54 – I Will Love the "Hard to Love" 156

Day 56 – I Will Be a Good Friend 159

Day 57 – I Will Run Well. 162

Day 58 – I Will Always Overcome 165

Day 59 – I Will Deny Myself 168

Day 60 – I Will Carry My Cross Daily. 171

Day 61 – I Will Live by Faith 174

Day 62 – I Will Speak Life 177

Day 63 – I Will Share My Testimony 179

About the Author. 181

INTRODUCTION

This devotional has been designed with one purpose: to renew your mind to a place of faith in all areas of life. I have read many devotionals that catered to the flesh, made me feel better for a moment, and encouraged me with relatable Bible stories. While these can be effective for short-term encouragement, I can't remember a single devotional that changed my life.

This book is different. I believe in the power of the Word of God spoken out loud. There is something about speaking things into the atmosphere and declaring your faith, regardless of your circumstance. This daily devotional, which will take only three to five minutes of your time each morning, will give you a brand-new mind. How can I say this with such confidence? It's science. Now some of these prayers may seem repetitive, but in order to program something, repetition is not only necessary but of the highest importance. Imagine an Olympic athlete. They don't get better by doing one hundred different things. They get better by doing one or several things thousands and thousands of times, until it's second nature. This is what we will do with God's Word.

Dr. Caroline Leaf, a Christian neuroscientist, has proven that the brain creates neuropathways based on what it takes in. She has concluded that over the course of nine weeks (sixty-three days), your brain can literally be reprogrammed. Say that you have inclinations to fear or worry. Over the next nine weeks as we declare truth and uproot fear, your brain will begin to shrink the neuropathways that send signals to fear. You will move from a highway of fear to a city street, to a dirt road, to nothing at all. We will then begin to rebuild these neuropathways to have faith by declaring the Word of God over our lives. Soon, your dirt road of faith will become a city street, then a highway. You will automatically live from a place of faith because your brain will have literally been programmed to do so.

If this sounds too good to be true, it's not. The Bible tells us that Jesus is the Prince of Peace (Isaiah 9:6), and that God gives us peace that surpasses knowledge and understanding (Philippians 4:6). It says that we can have joy everlasting (Isaiah 51:11), and that we haven't been given a spirit of fear, but of power love and a sound mind (2 Timothy 1:7). We are further told to cast all our cares, anxieties, and worries on Him because He cares for us (1 Peter 5:7). Have you ever wondered how to cast your cares on Jesus? Then this is the devotional for you.

You may feel like you will not overcome. Maybe right now, life seems to be overcoming you. If you feel like you need someone to talk to, or if you're considering taking your own life or have thought of doing so recently, please contact my friends at www.stayhere.live. There is a help line where someone will speak to you 24/7. You can also follow them on Instagram @stayhere.live for more uplifting content. You are not alone. Don't end your life. Stay here!

There are only four instructions for this book:

1) Read the prayer out loud. You are going to speak this truth of God's Word into the atmosphere. You are going to declare God's promises over your life for all the world and creation to bear witness to. There is also something about speaking things out loud in faith that creates more faith.

2) Don't stop praying just because you finished reading the prayer for the day. This devotional is meant to accomplish several things, one of them being to teach you how to pray truth over yourself. This type of prayer is led by the Holy Spirit and is rooted in biblical truth. Once you finish the written prayer, take another minute (or hour if you feel led) and let the Holy Spirit guide you. He may have more He wants you to declare or that He wants to reveal to you. As you finish reading the prayer, close your eyes and continue to pray out loud, and watch how He leads you. Build your prayer life day by day, and watch at the end of this book how much it grows.

3) Remember the title for that day's devotional reading (write it down somewhere or take a picture of it with your phone) and throughout the day, repeat it out loud. You may want to set an alarm to remind you to confess this powerful truth with your mouth. This declaration will help rewire your brain.

4) Write a review (on Amazon preferably) of the book and share how it impacted you. I want the world to know that it is possible to break free from anxiety, worry, depression, and fear by simply declaring truth over yourself in the name of Jesus. I believe you will overcome, and I want to hear about how you did.

Are you ready? Let's dive in.

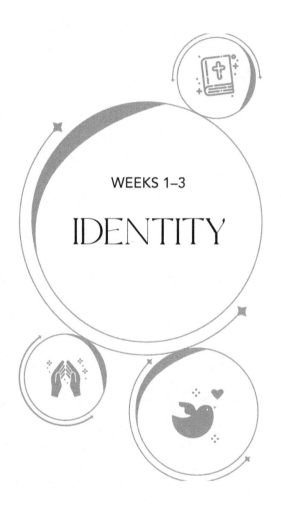

WEEKS 1–3

IDENTITY

Day 1

I Am Made in God's Image

BIBLICAL TRUTH

So God created man in his own image, in the image of God created He him; male and female created He them.

Genesis 1:27

The truth about your life is that you were created by God in His very image—in His likeness. The world will try to force different identities on you, or tell you who you should be or how you need to change to be liked or accepted. God isn't saying those things. He knows the image He made you in. But because of sin, that image was lost. As a result, every person, since the days of Adam and Eve, was born in need of love, and those who try to find it in the world will end up looking nothing like they were created to look.

Maybe you find yourself in that place right now. But know this: Jesus Christ came to earth to pay the penalty for our sin and restore our access to our Father in heaven. The blood of Jesus removes the sin of those who call upon His name. Now we have the ability to seek God and can find our true identity. Regardless of what life, the world, or the enemy is speaking to you today, rest in the truth of God's Word, which says you were made by Him, and He was pleased with His creation.

PRAYER

Father, I thank you in the name of Jesus for this day. I thank you that today I belong to you. I am yours, and you are my Lord, my Master, and my Savior. I thank you that you have created me in your image, and you did not make a mistake when you made me. I thank you, God, that day by day, you are shaping and molding me into the image of your Son, Jesus. I yield to you today completely and give you full permission to use me for your glory. I ask you to reveal to me anything inside of me that is not like you, so that I can give it to you. Father, I ask that you would speak to me. I pray today that you would help me see more and more who you are, so that I can learn who I am. I know that I will always overcome because of you. In Jesus' name I pray, amen.

Day 2

I Am
Loved by God

BIBLICAL TRUTH

> But God demonstrates His own love toward us, in
> that while we were still sinners, Christ died for us.
>
> Romans 5:8

"Jesus loves you!" We've heard this (I hope) so many
times throughout our lives, but what does it actually
mean? Because of the sinful nature we are born into, we
cannot get anywhere near God. He is so holy, so perfect, so
righteous, that we cannot enter His presence as sinners. The
Bible even says in Colossians 1:21 that our sin makes us
enemies of God. Wow.

But here's how much He loves us: He sent His only Son
to die on a cross so that we could be forgiven. *That* is love.
Even while we were sinners and enemies of God, He loved
us. We didn't deserve this love, and we certainly didn't and
never could earn it, but He gave it to us anyway. The world
might call you unlovable, or unworthy of love, but God has
already proven how worthy of love you are—not because of

anything you've done, but because of what Jesus has done. Let today be one when you remember what He did for you. He died so that you could live, and He did it all because of love. That is our King.

PRAYER

God, I thank you in the name of Jesus for loving me. I ask that, today, you would help me see more clearly how to receive your love. I think of who I've been in my past and who I would be without you, and all I can say is thank you. Thank you for choosing me even when I hadn't chosen you. Thank you for loving me first, before I was even created. Today, I want to be so aware of your love for me that I am changed from the inside out. I pray that you would help me show your love to everyone I meet. You loved me when I didn't deserve it, and I pray you will help me do the same to those all around me. I love you, God, and I give this day to you. Thank you that I will always overcome with you in me. In Jesus' name I pray, amen.

Day 3

I Am Who
God Says I Am

> And you, who once were alienated and enemies in
> your mind by wicked works, yet now He has rec-
> onciled in the body of His flesh through death, to
> present you holy, and blameless, and above reproach
> in His sight.
>
> Colossians 1:21–22

What would be a few words you would use to describe
yourself? Would *holy*, *blameless*, or *righteous* be on
that list? Well, that's what God thinks of you. This passage
above is one of my favorites because it paints a picture of
the gospel. We were cut off from God, enemies, wicked
in our nature, but He chose to make us right with Him
through His Son, Jesus Christ.

Now, because of the finished work of Jesus on the cross,
those of us who trust in Him are presented to God as holy,
blameless, and above reproach (of extreme integrity, perfect,
righteous). How amazing is that? We deserve death and hell

because of sin, and Jesus chose to not only forgive our sin and save us from death, but to present us to His Father as righteous. From sinners to right with God, all because of Christ. What a trade-off. Today, as you go, remember who God says you are, and remember that it is all because of the cross of Christ. Live in a place of thankfulness, and don't let the enemy or the world speak any other identity over you.

PRAYER

God, I thank you in the name of Jesus for loving me. I ask that, today, you would help me see more clearly how to receive your love. I think of who I've been in my past and who I would be without you, and all I can say is thank you. Thank you for choosing me even when I hadn't chosen you. Thank you for loving me first, before I was even created. Today, I want to be so aware of your love for me that I am changed from the inside out. I pray that you would help me show your love to everyone I meet. You loved me when I didn't deserve it, and I pray you will help me do the same to those all around me. I love you, God, and I give this day to you. I know I will always overcome. In Jesus' name I pray, amen.

God Desires Me

BIBLICAL TRUTH

> "And the glory which You gave Me I have given
> them, that they may be one just as We are one: I in
> them, and You in Me; that they may be made perfect
> in one, and that the world may know that You have
> sent Me, and have loved them as You have loved Me."
>
> John 17:22–23

In John 17 we see Jesus praying before He is to be
crucified. Jesus was preparing to face the most cruel,
painful, and torturous death that anyone in the history
of humanity would ever face. The Bible even says that
He was marred more than any of the sons of man, beaten
unrecognizable. Knowing this would be His fate, He still
took time to pray to His Father. In this prayer, He longs
for us to know God the way that He did, and for us to
be one with Him. The purpose of this oneness: *"that the
world may know that you have sent Me."* You were meant
to be one with God. You are loved by God and by His
Son, Jesus.

Jesus thought of you before He went to the cross. You were on His mind and in His heart. Today, know that you are seen, known, and loved by the God of the universe. You were created on purpose by someone who deeply desires to know you. Let His love consume you today and shape you into who you were always meant to be.

PRAYER

God, thank you for loving me. I thank you for sending your Son, Jesus, for me. Jesus, thank you for choosing me, and saying yes to me even while I was a sinner. Thank you, Jesus, for thinking of me before you went to the cross. Today I give myself to you. You are the potter and I am the clay, and I submit myself into the hands of the Master Potter. Shape and mold me, make me into something beautiful. Smooth out my rough edges and help me to see the way you see, so that I can love the way you love. I desire oneness with you. I ask you to fill me with the knowledge of you and your love, that the world may know you are real, that I am yours, and that you really sent Jesus to die for us all. Jesus, you live inside of me and today I receive your love. I don't need a thing from the world, because I've gotten everything I need from you. You saved me and made me new. Thank you. I know I will always overcome with you. In your name, amen.

Day 5

I Am Found

BIBLICAL TRUTH

> "For the Son of Man has come to seek and to save that which was lost."

Luke 19:10

Jesus came to save something that was lost, and it wasn't heaven. We aren't saved to go to heaven. What was lost was relationship, fellowship, communion, and access to our Creator. Sin entered the world in the garden of Eden; our perfect communion with God, the way He designed it, now had been broken. The Old Testament shows us the striving that took place to try to live righteously by fulfilling the law, but none could do it. Living from a place of striving is tiring; it wears you out. You're constantly trying to earn, constantly in a state of test taking, and constantly grading your own score.

Often, Christians condemn themselves based on their own grading system, instead of seeing that God grades our lives totally differently than we do. While our lives lived in faith and in obedience matter to God, they are not what earns us salvation. We do not get more love from God by "being good." We are saved by grace through faith in Christ alone. We are made righteous by the blood of Jesus alone. We are transformed from darkness to light because of Jesus. From that place of transformation, begin to thank God today. He has made you a brand-new creation. You are no longer lost but have been found. God is working on you daily, and He's not in a hurry. The Bible says we work out our salvation daily, so let's allow God to do His work in us day by day. Yield to Him today.

PRAYER

God, today I thank you that I once was lost but now I am found. Thank you for loving me, even at my worst. In my darkest moment, you saw me and never changed your mind about me. Thank you, Jesus, for choosing the cross so that I could have new life. Today, I want everything that comes from a relationship with you. Help me to see you clearly. I can look back on my life and see who I was, who I am now, and who I'm becoming. Thank you for never giving up on me. I know that I will always overcome because of you. I love you. In Jesus' name, amen.

Day 6

I Am His Joy

BIBLICAL TRUTH

> Let us run with endurance the race that is set before
> us, looking unto Jesus, the author and finisher of
> our faith, who for the joy that was set before Him
> endured the cross.
>
> Hebrews 12:1–2

If you meditate on this verse, it can change your life.
I grew up knowing that God loved me, because I was
always told that, but I also had this impression of Him
and Jesus as upset with me. I was very aware that my sin
put Jesus on the cross, and without this verse in my life, I
felt like Jesus went to that cross upset with me. I felt like
God was fed up with me and my junk, and Jesus had to
die so that the screwed-up version of me could be forgiven.
While it is true that our sin needs to be forgiven and we
must be born again, the motivation for Jesus going to the
cross was never expressed openly enough. He was *joyful.*
Jesus saw you and me and *chose* the cross. He was born to
die. He was born in pursuit of death on that cross, because
it meant He would purchase our lives with His blood, and

those of us who believe in Him would have the right to become children of God.

Know today that you were the joy set before Jesus. He knew what He was getting when He chose that death on the cross. No one drug Jesus to the cross and killed Him. He went of His own accord. He gave His life freely so that you could find yours. The nails didn't keep Him up there on that cross; His love for you did. The Bible even says that it pleased God to bruise His Son, because He knew He'd be getting you in return (Isaiah 53:10).

PRAYER

God, today I am so thankful for you. I'm thankful that you said my life was worth the blood of your Son. Jesus, I'm thankful that you lost your life so that I could find mine. How can it be that the most perfect man who ever lived would lay down His life for me? All I can say is thank you. You've shown me that I am so valuable to you. Today, help me to walk in the truth of my identity. I am not worthless. I am not a bother to you. I am not a burden to you. You are not disgusted with me or mad at me, but madly in love with me. Thank you for loving me today, God. I'm loved by you with no strings attached, no conditions, no expectations. Help me to walk in that freedom today so that I can love others in the same way. I know I will always overcome because of you, Jesus. In your name I pray, amen.

Day 7

I Am Forgiven, Not Condemned

BIBLICAL TRUTH

> "For God did not send His Son into the world to condemn the world, but that the world through Him might be saved."
>
> John 3:17

Christians can be some of the most condemned people on the planet, and many whom I meet are wrestling with real shame and guilt. The root of this problem is an unhealthy and incorrect view of God, and of ourselves. When we are born again, we are transferred from darkness into light. We are literally made into a new creation, something that has never existed before. The Bible says that our sins are forgiven and forgotten. They are thrown into the sea of forgetfulness, remembered no more, scattered as far as the east is from the west. This is because the blood of Jesus doesn't just forgive sin but cleanses it—removes it entirely.

When we are washed in His blood, we are made holy, blameless, and righteous in the sight of God. If we miss the mark of love and we sin, His grace is there to cover us. And Romans 5:23 lets us know that wherever sin is, there is more grace to cover it. Know today that God doesn't condemn you for not being perfect. Yes, He has called you to live like Jesus did and empowered you to do it. But know that His love for you is so great that His grace covers you in the times that you fall short. Don't live condemned today. God is a good Father who picks you up and dusts you off when you miss the mark. Keep burning for Him.

PRAYER

God, I thank you for loving me. Today, I choose by faith to believe that you aren't mad at me. You have spared me from hell because of your love. I thank you that your grace covers my shortcomings. I thank you that you have called me higher, to live righteously. I choose today to live by your Word and according to your commandments. I want to honor you because I love you too. Jesus, you said those who really loved you would keep your commands. Help me to do that today. I thank you that if I mess up, you're not going to send me to hell or banish me from your presence, but that your grace and mercy pull me out of the ruts I find myself in. I never want to abuse your grace to live however I want. I want to live for you because I love you. I choose to let your love motivate me to keep shining brightly for you, and to help me stay away from evil. I love you, God, and I know that I will always overcome because of you. In Jesus' name I pray, amen.

Day 8

I Am
a New Creation

BIBLICAL TRUTH

> Therefore, if anyone is in Christ, he is a new creation;
> old things have passed away; behold, all things have
> become new.
>
> 2 Corinthians 5:17

Sometimes as believers, we find ourselves remembering the things we did in our past. Whether it was the poor decisions we made, the people we may have hurt, or the addictions we may have walked through, humans have no shortage of trials. The enemy loves to remind you of where you've been and what you did. You can know it's the voice of the enemy because it will always be accompanied by shame or reasons to disqualify you from serving God. "Don't put your hands up in worship, you know what you did. Don't go pray for that person, you sinned earlier. You can't pray for anyone for a few days until you clean yourself up." These are some lies that the enemy loves to speak to you to try to get you to stop living in your identity.

But these are lies. You are a new creation. You aren't the person you were before. When you are born again, you are made into someone who has never existed before, and your sins are erased. If you sin as a believer, confess it to God and let His grace and mercy wash your conscience clean. Let His lovingkindness lead you to a life where you don't ever want to choose sin. But know this: as you're walking out this life with Him and working out your salvation day by day, you are forgiven. You are brand new. You are loved by God. He's not up in heaven waiting for you to mess up so He can punish you. He's cheering you on. And if you stray from the narrow path, He's there to guide you back onto it like the good Father that He is. Live free from regret today. Because of Christ and Christ alone, you're not who you used to be.

PRAYER

Father, I thank you today for making me a new creation. I remember who I used to be, stuck in sin and living for myself, but you saved me. You made me someone who's never existed before. Jesus, you paid the price on the cross for me to become one with you, and today I fully submit myself to you. I can see how you're working in me, Lord. I thank you that when I mess up, it hurts my heart because I love you so much and never want to sin or disobey. Keep me tender to your Word and to your commands. I love following you. Help me to see that you're not angry with me, but that you're Fathering me. I believe that I am who you say I am: forgiven and loved. Today, I live in faith that I am qualified because of your blood, Jesus. I will shine for you. I know I will always overcome with you. In your name I pray, amen.

Day 9

I Am Free
from Sin

BIBLICAL TRUTH

> Our old man was crucified with Him, that the body
> of sin might be done away with, that we should
> no longer be slaves of sin. For he who has died has
> been freed from sin.
>
> Romans 6:6–7

When was the last time someone told you that, as
a Christian, you were free from sin? I've heard it
preached many times that we are saved from hell, but
Jesus died to remove sin. John the Baptist didn't say,
"Behold, the Lamb of God who takes away hell." No, he
said "who takes away the sin of the world." See, Jesus'
blood on the cross removed sin and the penalty of sin,
which is death. Those who are born again are set free from
sin and its clutches. We no longer are slaves to it like we
were before we belonged to God. The Bible even says that
now we are slaves to something else—to righteousness. We
now wake up every day and wonder, *How can I serve God*

today? How can I love Him more? How can I show the world that He is real?

These are things we never thought about before as unbelievers, but now we do. The thought of changing the world around us for Jesus sometimes plagues us. It can even feel like a burden, like a chain of bondage. But it's a healthy burden, a chain to be desired. Oh, what a privilege to feel the burden of winning the lost for Christ and not being able to be satisfied with anything else. This is the mind of a believer who is burning with passion for Christ, not for sin. This doesn't mean you will never sin again. It means you don't have to. It's not a guarantee. You are no longer a slave to sin. Today, know that by the power of the cross of Christ alone you have been set free from sin, in order that you might go shine for Him to all people. You're not a slave to the devil any longer. He is defeated.

PRAYER

God, I thank you today that you love me. I thank you, Jesus, that because of what you did on the cross, I have been eternally set free from sin. Without you I'd be stuck in my old ways, living for myself and living for the world. Thank you, Father, that today I am free to worship, serve, and love you with every fiber of my being. I want to live a life that honors you, and I thank you for setting me free so that I can. I am no longer a slave to sin, or to the devil, but now a slave to righteousness. I no longer have to do what my flesh wants to do, or what the enemy invites me to do, but I can live by the Spirit.

Thank you for loving me so much that even while I was a sinner, you came and paid the price for me to be set free. Today, I honor you and worship you as the one who broke off my heavy chains of bondage and made me brand new. I love you, God, and I live for you today and always, and I know I will always overcome with you. In Jesus' name, amen.

I Am a Saint, Not a Sinner

BIBLICAL TRUTH

> But you are a chosen generation, a royal priesthood,
> a holy nation, His own special people, that you may
> proclaim the praises of Him who called you out of
> darkness into His marvelous light.
>
> 1 Peter 2:9

Have you ever heard another Christian say, "Well, you
know, we're all broken sinners who need Jesus"? They
say that we are (still) sinners, saved by grace. The truth is
that we *were* sinners who needed Jesus—until we were born
again. Now we are saints who need Jesus. The Bible makes
it very clear that sin and the identity as a sinner are things
that died with the "old man"—the things that were crucified with Christ when you became brand new. Your sinful
nature is dead and there's a new nature in its place.

You can't get born again and still be the same person.
Because of the blood of Jesus Christ and your faith in
Him, you have been transformed from death to life, from

darkness to light, from sinner to saint. This doesn't mean you're perfect or that you're sinless. What it does mean is that sin is no longer your identity. If you see yourself as a sinner, there's a good chance you'll start to live like one. If you see yourself as a saint, you'll protect your heart from the things of the world and serve God in purity. Right now, you stand before God as holy, blameless, and righteous because of Jesus' work on the cross. Don't wear your old identity as a sinner. Wear the identity Jesus paid for you to have.

PRAYER

Father, I thank you in Jesus' name for giving me a new identity. I ask today that you help me to see myself the way that you see me. I choose by faith to believe that I am holy, righteous, and blameless in your sight because of what Jesus did on the cross. Thank you, Jesus, for paying that price for me. You have set me free from sin and death, and I live today to honor you. I thank you that I'm no longer a sinner. I have been called out of darkness and into your marvelous light. Thanks for putting your love and light inside of me. Help me to shine everywhere I go today. Help me to remember who I am because of you. I see how you're working in me and making me more like you every day. I see how free I am compared to when I first met you, and I can only say thank you. I know you're working in me, even in ways that I can't see. I yield myself to you today and ask you to reveal to me more and more the freedom that you paid for me to walk in. I love you, Lord, and today I choose to believe what you say. I will always overcome with you, Jesus. In your name, amen.

Day 11

I Am Not a Mistake

BIBLICAL TRUTH

> For You formed my inmost being; You knit me
> together in my mother's womb. I praise You, for I am
> fearfully and wonderfully made.
>
> Psalm 139:13–14

I once read Psalm 139 three times a day for a week. By the end of the week I couldn't finish the whole thing without breaking down in tears. There is something so powerful about declaring it over yourself, and these two verses show the intentionality God had when He made you and me. The psalmist praises God because of how much He cares for us. The best part about God's Word is that it's always the same, and always true. Despite what kind of upbringing you had, how your parents were or weren't, or whether you even had parents or not, it doesn't dictate who God says you are and it doesn't determine your value.

God made you on purpose. You weren't a mistake or an accident. God knew what He was doing when He made you in your mother's womb. The world may look at the circumstances surrounding your birth or your childhood and tell you how valuable or unvaluable you are. God looks at you, in the middle of all of your mess, and says, "You are my creation. You are my child. I love you. I made you for a purpose, and I sacrificed my own Son so that I could have you." The truth is that you may have made some mistakes, but that doesn't make you one. Live today knowing you were God's idea, and He called you wonderful.

PRAYER

God, thank you that you love me. Thank you for giving me another day to shine for you. I know that I woke up on purpose, because you have more for me in this life. I believe that my life matters to you, and that you did not make a mistake when you created me. I thank you that even though my life has not been perfect, I have everything I need because you live inside of me. Today, I choose to believe by faith that I am not an accident. You formed me in my mother's womb. You saw my unformed body, long before the world was ever formed. You thought of me before the beginning of time, and you loved me. You saw me when I was at my worst and lowest point in my life, and you never changed your mind about me. You never regretted creating me or giving me life. Thank you, Jesus, that my life means so much to you, that you laid yours down. Thank you, God, that in you and you alone, I can find my life. Today, I live for you on purpose, because I was created on purpose. I love you, Lord, and I know I will always overcome with you. I pray these things in Jesus' name, amen.

Day 12

My Life
Has Purpose

BIBLICAL TRUTH

"For I know the thoughts that I think toward you,
says the Lord, thoughts of peace and not of evil, to
give you a future and a hope."

Jeremiah 29:11

Maybe you've asked yourself, *What's my purpose? Why
am I alive?* Finding your purpose in this life might
seem like trying to find a needle in a haystack. I know in
my own life, this question came up over and over again as
I progressed through high school and college, and as an
Army officer, a police officer, and now a missionary. I was
constantly asking God why He put me on the earth. I know
now that my purpose is to win the lost to Christ.

Do you know your purpose? If you do, this verse should
encourage you to remember that God is the one who's
desire is to give you a future and a hope. Rest in Him as you
pursue your calling. Maybe you don't know your purpose

just yet. Rest in the truth that God has something for you. You're not without hope. There is a future for you that God is orchestrating. Lean on Him and don't fret or let anxiety set in. Don't believe the lie that there's no purpose for your life, as if you're the one God missed or forgot about. He is thinking of you today, and His thoughts are good.

PRAYER

Lord, thank you for your love for me. I believe that you think about me and have plans for my life. I believe that you haven't forgotten about me or left me without a future or a hope. Thank you, Lord, for giving me life. I repent for any times that I've tried to take life into my own hands. I recognize that every time I try to do this, I allow anxiety and worry to set in. Father, I thank you that you deliver me from all fear and anxiety. I am free by the blood of Jesus. Today I walk in freedom, and I surrender my plans, my will, and my desires to you. God, I trust you. I believe that the plans you have for me are much greater than any plans I could ever have for myself. I believe that the things you're saying over me are for my good, for peace, and are hopeful. I rebuke every thought of evil that comes against me, and I recognize that it is not from you, God. I will not allow evil thoughts to take up any space in my mind. I choose today, by faith, to believe your Word over my emotions and over my circumstances. Thanks for loving me, God. I love you and I will follow you forever. I will always overcome. In Jesus' name, amen.

Day 13

I Live by the Spirit

BIBLICAL TRUTH

> For to be carnally minded is death, but to be spiritually minded is life and peace.
>
> Romans 8:6

As Christians, we have been gifted with a Helper, a Comforter, an Advocate and Friend. The Holy Spirit is the Spirit of God Himself, living within us. The problem in today's world is that many people either don't know about the Holy Spirit or don't understand His role in our lives. I've heard Him talked about as a "thing" or an "it," but He is a person. He is God.

The Bible makes it clear that living according to the Holy Spirit is life and peace. The opposite of living by the Spirit is living by the flesh, which is sensual and demonic. Without the Holy Spirit working within us, we would continue living as we did before we were born again—living according to how we feel, what we want or think we need, or by what pleases us. Living this way is selfish in nature and leads only to destruction. The Bible goes as far as to say that living according to the flesh is hostile toward God (Romans 8:7).

However, if we choose to live by the Spirit, we can experience life and life more abundantly. The Holy Spirit will guide us into all truth, show us the way to live, and empower us to do it. This life will result in life and peace in your heart, not destruction and anxiety. God is constantly speaking to us through His Holy Spirit. It might come in the form of thoughts, dreams, or visions. Are you listening for Him? Live by the Spirit today and listen for God to speak to you.

PRAYER

God, I thank you for giving me your Holy Spirit. Thank you for giving me a Helper, a Comforter, and someone to look out for me. I praise you, God, that you have not left me without help or without power but have put your Spirit inside of me. Today, I want to walk step by step with your Spirit. I want to hear you speak to me. I ask you to lead and guide me today. I thank you for conviction in my life, that when I am straying from the narrow path you are faithful to lead me back by your Spirit. Thank you for teaching me, loving me, and Fathering me. I believe that in you is life and peace, and I surrender myself to you today. Show me the life you have for me. Lead me into your peace. I rest in your promises over my life, and I yield to your guidance. Holy Spirit, I ask you to fill me right now to complete the assignment you have for me. I will always overcome with you, Jesus. In your name, amen.

Day 14

I Am Not My Circumstances

BIBLICAL TRUTH

For we walk by faith, not by sight.

2 Corinthians 5:7

Though short, this verse has enough truth in it to change the way you live your life. For most people in the world, sight is how they live. It seems almost ignorant to the majority of the world to live contrary to what is seen. To them, the things that are seen are tangible, and can be observed with the senses; it's a form of evidence. To tell someone to not let what is seen dictate your life, but rather put faith in God, who is unseen, sounds absurd. This verse actually goes deeper than just an overall concept of having faith that God will work things out over the span of your life, but actually choosing to have faith, on purpose, in every situation.

Imagine you got alerted at work that the company was going to be laying off 25 percent of the workers next month due to budget cuts. You choose to have faith in that moment instead of living analytically, which would have you worrying about numbers, your position in the company, who you're "in" with and what strings you might pull, and so on. Now, some of those things can be helpful in keeping your job, but if your faith is in yourself, then God gets no glory. And, if your faith is in your own hands, you have the ability to fail.

People in these situations often face anxiety and worry. Why? Because humans fail all the time. But God never does. It's possible to hear that news and say, "Lord, I know this doesn't look good, and 25 percent is a lot of people, but I trust in you. Help me to do the best I can to show my value at this company. If it is your will, I would love to keep this job. If you have something else for me, even though I don't understand or know what it is, I trust you. I can't lose in this position because you are for me. Thanks, God."

Let's live by faith, not sight, today.

PRAYER

God, thank you for loving me today. Thank you that you've given me your Spirit, and because of you, I have been set free from myself. I am not at the mercy of my circumstances today, but am filled with hope, faith, joy, and love. Today, I choose by faith to see the way you see. I look at every situation I encounter as an opportunity to shine for you—and show the world that you're really real and that you live inside of me. Thank you for empowering me to always overcome the trials and issues of life. I will always overcome with you, Jesus. I pray this in your name, amen.

Day 15

No One Owes Me Anything

BIBLICAL TRUTH

The Lord is my shepherd; I shall not want.

Psalm 23:1

I remember memorizing this verse as a young boy in the AWANA program at my church. I would blaze through it, totally skipping over the semicolon, because usually the faster I could recite a verse, the less likely the chance of my messing it up. The older I get, the more I realize how important the second part of that verse is: "I shall not want." Another translation says, "I don't need a thing" (MSG). How true this is. But my fear and what breaks my heart is that many around the world do not hold this verse as a truth. And for many, even if it is regarded as a truth, it hasn't become a revelation.

The Word of God is meant to transform, not simply inform. If we truly meditated on this verse, we could be at peace. Living from a place of believing, by faith, that the Lord is not only your leader and your guide, but that He completely

36

supplies for your every need, can change your life. The world tells you that you have many needs and desires, and that it has the answer for you to be fulfilled. God's Word says the opposite. What if we lived a life where we believed God, even when it didn't make sense to our flesh? Today, let's declare that God is enough. Your every need is seen by Him and won't go unmet. If He provides for the birds of the air, surely He will provide for you, His child.

PRAYER

God, thank you for being my provider. Thanks for loving me and making me more like you day by day. I admit that there are times when I am tempted to worry. There are times in my life where I'm tempted to look at my circumstances, or find areas of my life that I would describe as lacking, and worry. Today, I repent of worrying about anything. I declare, by faith, that today I trust in you. You have never failed me, and I know you never will. God, help me see the areas of my life that I have tried to do on my own, so that I can surrender them to you. Help me to submit everything to you, and free me from all worry and anxiety. I come out of agreement with fear of the unknown. I will not fear because you, God, see me, love me, and know me. I trust in you to be my provider at all times. I receive this verse over my life, that today I can live in a place where I declare that you are my guide, and I don't need anything else. Thank you for loving me and saving me. I know that in you, I will always overcome. In Jesus' name I pray, amen.

Day 16

I Am Not Alone

BIBLICAL TRUTH

"And He will give you another Helper, that He may abide with you forever."

John 14:16

Isolation is one of the many tools of the enemy during a trial. Whether it's in temptation or tribulation, the enemy loves to get us alone, because he knows that the power of unity and agreement are devastating to his kingdom and his attacks. I fully believe in the power of community to break off chains, push back darkness, and overcome tough situations, but let us not forget that it is not our community that keeps us from being alone.

We have the Holy Spirit living inside of us. As I discussed earlier in this book, He is a person. He's not an "it" or an "idea," but God Himself in Spirit form, living within us. The enemy's biggest tactic when fear sets in is to make us feel like we're all alone. As Christians, we must combat the lies of the enemy with the Word of God. What if the next time you were tempted or tried, you responded out loud with, "God, thank you that you're with me right now. I am not alone,

I don't have to face this alone, and I will always overcome because you are with me. Thank you for loving me."

These simple declarative statements of faith, which are actually the Word of God in a short prayer, are so powerful. The enemy cannot stand against a Christian who is fully submitted to the Holy Spirit within them. Today, know that Jesus promised He would give us the Spirit, and that He would never leave us. Today and forever, you are not alone.

PRAYER

God, thank you for the gift of your Holy Spirit in my life. I believe that you are actually living inside of me. You're not just some "being" up in the clouds, but you're here, right now, in me and with me always. Your name is Emmanuel, "God with us," "God with me." I ask that you give me more revelation of what it means to walk with you at all times. Open my eyes to see you in every situation, in every environment, at all times. All I desire is to know you and worship you with my life. I repent for any times that I've acted out of fear or believed the lie that I was alone. I believe your Word. I believe that you are with me and that you'll never leave or forsake me. Today, I turn my ears toward your voice, and my eyes toward your face. Speak to me, lead me and guide me. You are my God, my Helper, my Comforter, my Friend. Holy Spirit, thank you for filling me and making your home inside of me. I know that with you, I will always overcome. I pray these things in the name of Jesus, amen.

Day 17

I Was Made to Shine

BIBLICAL TRUTH

> For it is the God who commanded light to shine out of darkness, who has shone in our hearts to give the light of the knowledge of the glory of God in the face of Jesus Christ.
>
> 2 Corinthians 4:6

> In the midst of a crooked and perverse generation, among whom you shine as lights in the world.
>
> Philippians 2:15

This verse has been wrecking me over the last year. The idea that the God of the universe, the One who created everything, has shone in my heart and yours. Ugh. I think of Psalm 8:4: "What is man, that you are mindful of him?" God desires to know us and love us, but it doesn't stop there. He actually wants to use us to further His Kingdom. God shows Himself within us, because it brings glory to Him. All this is done because people see Jesus in us and determine that God is real. What a privilege.

Couple this with the verse from Philippians 2, and you have your purpose on this earth: to shine. We live in a crooked and perverse generation, but we were called to light up the darkness. God has put His light inside of us, and now we have the great honor of showing that light to the world, who desperately needs it. Today, you may encounter darkness, or you may already be walking through it, but know that you are well equipped. Go into the dark places with confidence, in faith, because the Light of the World is inside of you.

PRAYER

God, thank you for loving me. Thank you for putting your light inside of me. I believe what your Word says, that you desire to use me to shine, and to be a light to my generation. I ask that you give me your heart for those around me who don't know you. I never want to be someone who complains about the darkness, when I have the very solution living within me. I repent of any time that I've been pessimistic about my generation, my coworkers, my friends, or my family. I see that you've placed me on this earth for such a time as this, and that you have empowered me to bring the Kingdom everywhere I go. Help me to realize today the authority that you've placed inside of me to speak to darkness and command it to flee in the name of Jesus. Help me to walk in love, not considering my own desires, but putting others above myself. Help me to be a person who sees You in every situation. Help me to be someone who thinks the best of people, hopes all

41

things, and doesn't complain. I repent for complaining, because I realize that it's rooted in selfishness, and I can't shine outward if I'm looking inward. I love you, God, and I know that I'll always overcome the darkness with your light inside of me. In Jesus' name I pray, amen.

I Am Qualified by Him

BIBLICAL TRUTH

> Giving thanks to the Father who has qualified us to be partakers of the inheritance of the saints in the light.
>
> Colossians 1:12

As we grow up in this world, we become used to the idea of either being qualified or unqualified to do something. Whether in school, on a team, or in the workplace, we are no strangers to having to prove ourselves or earn our spot. We have to convince the teacher, the coach, or the boss that we have value and can add to the organization. It shouldn't be any surprise that most Christians I've met who struggle with insecurity, view God this same way. God is often seen as this "being" or even as a judge, high up in the clouds, sitting in a court room with a large gavel, waiting to sentence us favorably (we hope) or unfavorably. We believe we can affect God's demeanor by our actions, which leads to striving to earn His attention, affection, and love.

When we do this, we open ourselves up to, once again, grade our own test and say whether God likes us today or not. This leaves many Christians feeling depressed, worried, and hopeless. The truth is this: God is not like that. You cannot earn a spot on God's "team." You are qualified because of what Jesus has done. You have been given the right to become a child of God because of the finished work of the cross of Christ. Rest today in the knowledge that God deeply loves you and said yes to you long before you were even created. You are qualified to be loved and saved by God, because He said you were before the foundation of the earth.

PRAYER

God, thank you so much for calling me your own. You loved me before the foundation of the world, before I was born or even knew who you were. You loved me when I was a sinner. You have never changed your mind about me, and you've always seen who I was created to be. Thank you for your Son who died for me so that I could know you. I rest today in the knowledge that you have qualified me to partake in your glory. You have made me a new creation and set me apart. You've seated me in heavenly places and removed the stain of my sin. You've washed me clean and given me a new heart. You've called me a co-heir with Christ. Jesus, thank you for sharing your inheritance with me. I repent for ever striving or trying to earn your love or attention. I recognize that you aren't like the people of this world. Help me to trust you. Help me to believe your Word and know that you have always loved me and always will. I choose by faith to walk in that freedom today, and I know that with you I will always overcome. In the name of Jesus I pray, amen.

I Was Made to Love

BIBLICAL TRUTH

> "A new commandment I give to you, that you love one another; as I have loved you, that you also love one another. By this all will know that you are My disciples, if you have love for one another."
>
> John 13:34–35

Do you remember hearing about the Ten Commandments in Sunday School? I hope it was in the context of the old law, because we don't live by those commandments anymore. We aren't under the old law. Jesus stated that the old covenant with Moses, which consisted of the Ten Commandments and 613 Laws of the Prophets, were fulfilled by His work on the cross.

Jesus said He didn't come to do away with the law but to complete it. Now, we have new assignments, but by doing them we actually fulfill everything previously written. We are to love God with everything inside of us, and to love our neighbor as ourselves. Jesus says all the laws hang on these two, because love does no harm to a neighbor. Love is the answer. Jesus then adds this new commandment: love one another the same way that He loved us. He says the intention of this is that the world will know we belong to Him. You were created to love, and by that love, the world will know that He is real. Today, love those around you on purpose.

PRAYER

Father, I thank you for loving me. I thank you that your Word, which says that you loved me before the world was formed, is true, and that I love you as a response to that first love. You are my first love, God. I believe that I was created to be loved by you, and to reveal your love to the world, that they may know I belong to you. God, I repent of any time in my life that I haven't been loving. I admit that there have been times that I let something matter more than what matters most. I confess that sometimes it seems easier to cut someone out and isolate myself than it is to love, but I see that love is the true answer to unity. I want unity in my family, in my friend group, and in my nation. I ask you to use me today however you want to. I know that when I walk out my front door, I instantly have countless opportunities to love. Help me to not be a quiet Christian. I never want to be shy about our relationship. God, I'm asking you to break off any fear in my heart that would cause me to stay quiet about you. I ask you to rid me of any need to be accepted that would keep me from speaking about you or doing something kind for someone else because I'm worried about what it might look like. Thanks for never condemning me for where I'm not, but calling me to a higher place. I'm ready and willing to be used by you. I know that with you, I will always overcome. I pray these things in your name, Jesus. Amen.

Day 20

I Have Something to Give

BIBLICAL TRUTH

> Then Peter said, "Silver and gold I do not have, but
> what I do have I give you: In the name of Jesus Christ
> of Nazareth, rise up and walk."
>
> Acts 3:6

This is such an amazing encounter. Peter and John were walking to the temple to pray, and near the gate was a man who was lame (he could not walk) since birth. Every day he would lie by the gate and beg for money. When Peter and John walked by, he looked at them expecting to receive something. Peter gave him something, all right. Peter was filled with the Holy Spirit and had been empowered to do what Jesus did. He gave this man the Kingdom of God, and the man was instantly healed. The man got up and began leaping and praising God, all the way into the temple.

Do you know that you have something to give as well? We who are Christians have the exact same Holy Spirit that Jesus had, the same Spirit that rose Him from the dead. We don't need an abundance of silver or gold. These are things that can't come with us when we die anyway. What we can bring with us to heaven are people. You have the opportunity and the authority to give the Kingdom of God to everyone you meet. Today, you might be lacking in earthly resources, but your access to the riches in heaven are unlimited and unrestricted. When you see someone in need, whether it's of physical healing in their body or emotional healing in their soul, give them the Kingdom. Lay your hands on them and pray in the name of Jesus for them to be healed. Oh, what a privilege we have to pray in the name of Jesus. Let's not take that for granted.

PRAYER

God, thank you for loving me today. Thank you that by your mercy, you've woken me up to have another chance to shine for you. I want to be used by you, like you used Peter to restore the beggar by the gates of the temple. I believe in you, God. I believe your Word, and that you have empowered me to give your Kingdom to a world that desperately needs it. I believe that you want to move through my hands, speak through my prayers, and love through my life to reach the world for your glory. Today, I surrender myself to you. I ask you to convict me of the chances in my life to love those that many might overlook, like the beggar in this passage. Wound my heart with a longing to share your Word with those in the world that seem to be unseen. I believe I have something to give because you live inside of me. I don't need money or resources because I am filled with your Spirit. Thank you for making your home in me. I know I will always overcome because of you. In Jesus' name I pray, amen.

I Am Not Afraid

BIBLICAL TRUTH

> For God has not given us a spirit of fear, but of power
> and of love and of a sound mind.
>
> 2 Timothy 1:7

When faced with an intense situation that requires an immediate action, our body goes into the "fight or flight" mode. Our basic survival instincts take over, and our minds and bodies do what they think needs to be done in order to keep us alive. This can be helpful at times, but detrimental in others. How would you feel if you were standing next to a police officer in a gas station store, and an armed gunman came in demanding money and the police officer ran away? It would be quite a scary situation for most, because we know that it is the police who exist to stop this very kind of person.

What do we do when our help is running for their own lives? When I served as a police officer in a dangerous city just south of Seattle, I was trained to run toward the danger and not away from it. As Christians, we have an even greater help than police training or being armed with a weapon. We have the Holy Spirit. The psalmist said in Psalm 44 that he doesn't trust in his bow or his sword, but in God to save. How true this is. God is our help. He has given us power. He has given us love. We have no reason to fear. And He has equipped us with a sound mind, capable of making clear decisions, without being overcome by emotions. Today, rest in the truth that whatever situation you are in, you can be at peace and respond with wisdom, not because of your own abilities but because of the Spirit of God living within you.

PRAYER

Father, I thank you today that you love me. I thank you for shaping me and molding me into the image of your Son. Thank you for choosing me long before the foundation of the world. You saw me, my unformed frame, and said yes to me. Thank you, God. I believe your Word. I believe that I can trust in you. I repent of any time that I've allowed fear to have a place in my life. I repent for ever partnering with the lies of the enemy that would cause me to panic or have anxiety. I repent for not trusting you. I thank you for leading me into truth today. I choose by faith to trust in you, even when I can't see the outcome or the process to get there. I choose to believe what you've spoken through your Word. You've never failed me, God. I've never been forsaken by you, and I know I never will. Right now, in the name of Jesus Christ, I command every bit of fear that is trying to remain in my life to leave. God,

I thank you that every evil and tormenting spirit that would bring fear has to go, in the name of Jesus. I come out of agreement with fear and into agreement with peace and hope in you. I have the spirit of power, love, and a sound mind living inside of me, and I will always overcome. In Jesus' name, amen.

WEEKS 4–6

AUTHORITY

Day 22

I Have the Same Spirit as Jesus Did

BIBLICAL TRUTH

But if the Spirit of Him who raised Jesus from the dead dwells in you, He who raised Christ from the dead will also give life to your mortal bodies through His Spirit who dwells in you.

Romans 8:11

This verse is one that should bring you such joy. How amazing is it that we have the exact same Spirit in us that Jesus had in Him? The same Spirit that rose Jesus from the dead is dwelling in you and me. It is crystal clear now why Jesus told us that we can pray and ask anything in His name, according to the will of God, and it shall be done. We have access to God through the Holy Spirit, and we have the power of God through Him as well. Jesus said in His name we will heal the sick, raise the dead, cast out demons, cleanse the lepers, and preach the gospel to the poor in spirit.

It is only by the Spirit of God that we can have the power to do any of these things. Of our own accord, we are powerless against the enemy and his works of darkness. But with the power of God through His Spirit, we can move mountains. When Peter told Jesus that He was the Christ, Jesus responded by letting him know that it was the Holy Spirit who told Peter that information. No one could know that or speak it without the Holy Spirit. Without the Spirit of God, Peter denied Jesus three times, just hours after saying he would die for Him. Later, after the Holy Spirit came upon the disciples in the upper room, Peter, then filled with the Spirit, began to boldly declare the resurrection of Jesus to the very people who crucified Him. Peter, who once feared for his life in the face of danger, was now confronting it. This was done because of the mighty power of the Holy Spirit in Him. Today, know that if you are a Christian and are born again, you have this same Spirit in you too. If you've never been filled with the Spirit, ask God right now. Say this: "God, I desire to know you more and follow you with my everything. Please fill me right now with your Holy Spirit, in the name of Jesus. Amen."

PRAYER

God, I thank you for loving me. I praise you for how mighty you are. You raised Jesus from the dead by the power of your Holy Spirit, and you have desired to make me a home for Him. Thank you, God, for putting your Spirit inside of me. I worship you for who you are. You are my God, my Master, my Savior, my Lord. Thank you for calling me a friend. Thank you for making me a temple for the Holy Spirit. I want to be used by you today. Lead me, by your Spirit, to pray for someone today, to lay hands on the sick, to share your Word with someone who needs encouragement. Use me however you want. I believe you want to speak to me today. I am listening for your voice in the quiet of my thoughts. Thank you for filling me with your love and your power. I know that I will always overcome because of you. In Jesus' name, amen.

God Wants to Use Me

BIBLICAL TRUTH

I beseech you therefore, brethren, by the mercies of
God, that you present your bodies a living sacrifice,
holy, acceptable to God, which is your reasonable
service. And do not be conformed to this world, but
be transformed by the renewing of your mind, that
you may prove what is that good and acceptable and
perfect will of God.

Romans 12:1–2

This verse has two separate charges in it that are important to grab onto. The first is this: we are called to be
living sacrifices. The second: to prove the will of God.
Those are pretty big, so let's break them down. First, to be a
living sacrifice means making the decision to lay down our
lives so that Christ can live through us. We must daily deny
ourselves and lay down our desires and our wills so that
God can do whatever He wants in us. Often, it's easy to get
caught up in our hopes and dreams, but how often do we

pause and ask God, "Do you like my job? Do you like my friend groups? Do you like my goals? What would you have me do, Lord?" How often do we present our lives, our day-to-day decisions and efforts, at the feet of Jesus?

When I began doing this in my life, I was shocked at how many areas He desired to change. I can say now, after years of walking with Jesus, that this way of living is the only way. I would gladly surrender my will for His, because I've seen His faithfulness time and time again. Second, we are called to prove the will of God. I've heard people say, "You can't know God's will. That's prideful to say." But the Bible makes it clear that God's will is no longer a mystery. He has revealed it through the life of Jesus, and here in Romans, Paul makes it obvious that a life surrendered to Jesus will result in being transformed. This transformation and renewing of our ways of thinking will prove to the world, and to ourselves, that God is real and is at work in the world. Today, make the decision to surrender to God so that He can work in you. Let Him use you fully. He wants to!

PRAYER

God, thank you for being my God. Thank you for loving me today. I honor you as Lord, and I am so thankful that you want to use me. I am humbled that the God of the universe, the God of all creation, wants to use me. Father, I submit myself to you today. I'm asking you to work in and through me. Show me what it really means to be a living sacrifice. I want to prove your perfect will on this earth to everyone I meet. I ask you to consume me. Wear me like a glove. I surrender my mind, body, will, and emotions to you today. I trust that you have better plans for me than I could ever have for myself. I trust that you know how to use me to further your Kingdom better than I do. I recognize that full surrender means trusting in you with my life, and I repent right now for any times I've tried to take my life into my own hands or pursue my own desires without seeking yours first. Thank you for showing me that there is a better way to live than trying to do it on my own. I believe that I will always overcome because of you living in me. In Jesus' name, amen.

I Can Hear God

BIBLICAL TRUTH

"My sheep hear My voice, and I know them, and they follow Me."

John 10:27

One of the biggest things I've noticed since I began preaching on social media is the vast amount of people who struggle with the idea that they can hear God speak to them. I've made videos about hearing God that have gotten millions of views and tens of thousands of comments, and the main comment is something to the effect of "I didn't know I could hear God." All I do in these videos is lead them in a prayer asking God to speak to them, and create a quiet space at the end for them to listen, and instruct them to comment the first thing that comes to their mind. Many of us pray and pray and pray, but never listen. The comments on these videos are amazing, as they realize for the first time that God will actually speak to them.

Most people think that when God speaks, it will be in a loud booming voice. While some people have heard an audible voice, even then they will tell you that it is a rare occasion. For the common Christian, hearing God comes in the form of a thought, an impression, a vision, or a dream. There are also prophetic words and words of knowledge given by others to us, but today we are focusing on your ability to hear God for yourself and for others. In my life, the primary way God speaks to me is through thoughts. Think about it this way: God lives inside of us through the dwelling of the Holy Spirit in our bodies. When God speaks to us through His Spirit, we receive the thought without the voice, because we are now the body of the Holy Spirit.

I remember standing in line at a Starbucks when I was a new believer and having the thought, *Pay for the person behind you.* It wasn't mean or harsh or like the voice of a dictator, but a kind thought that provoked me to love someone. I ended up paying for their order and blessing them, and when I left, I had another thought that said, *I want to use you to bless others.* This thought caught me off guard because it was directed *at* me. I remember thinking, *Wow. God is speaking to me right now.* Since that day, I have been listening for His still small voice every day, everywhere I go. At the end of today's prayer, sit quietly and listen for Him.

PRAYER

God, thank you for loving me and for putting your Spirit inside of me. I believe in you, and I know that you desire to speak to me. You said in your Word that your sheep will know your voice. I choose to believe today, by faith, that I can know your voice. Help me to listen for you every day. I will be mindful of you in all that I do. I will not get so busy in life that I don't give you space to speak to me. I ask you to lead and guide me by your voice. I want to be provoked by you to do acts of kindness for others. Help me to learn what you sound like. I am so thankful that prayer is not a one-way conversation. Right now, I ask you to speak to me. I'm listening for your voice, and I know I'll always overcome because you lead me through life. I love you and I praise you. In Jesus' name, amen.

Day 25

God Can Hear Me

BIBLICAL TRUTH

> "For from the first day that you set your heart to
> understand, and to humble yourself before your God,
> your words were heard."
>
> Daniel 10:12

Have you ever wondered if God hears your prayers? When I was younger, it used to feel like sometimes my prayers bounced off the ceiling and never made it to God. I also had a wrong view of God, that He was up in the clouds and hard to reach. I had heard that God is always with us, but that wasn't my revelation. This verse from Daniel filled me with such hope, to think that God hears me as soon as I open my mouth and is moving on my behalf, even if I might not see it right away.

When I got born again and started really diving into the Word and into places of deep prayer, I began to realize that I had grown up with a wrong view of the Father. God always hears my prayers. God is always listening to me. He never takes a day off or is unreachable. I saw the power of prayer over my life, as I began to declare the truth of God's Word over myself. I began to see how God would answer very specific prayers I had prayed—not for a nice car or a promotion, but prayers about knowing Him more, or for wisdom, or guidance. I remember looking back months after praying things like this and realizing God had given me these things. I saw areas in my life where I responded with wisdom that I previously would not have. I saw areas of my life where I was growing in patience, in kindness, in tenderheartedness, and in love. It was by reflecting that I could see how my prayers had been answered. The temptation in life is often to keep looking ahead for the next thing, but if you read the Old Testament, God constantly reminds the Israelites to look back at what He has done for them so that they never forget.

Today, in the midst of your planning and goal setting for the future, don't forget to look back and reflect on what God has done. You'll find that there are some prayers you used to pray that God has answered that you might have not even realized. Let's not get so caught up in asking God for things, that we forget to look back and see what He's already given us. When you see all God has done for you, you'll grow in confidence that He heard you when you prayed. If He's done it before, He will do it again.

PRAYER

> Father, I thank you that you love me and that you hear me when I pray. I believe in you. I believe you are who you say you are. I believe that your Word is true, and that when I call upon your name, you

hear me. Today, I ask you to help me reflect on my life. Show me all the areas where you've answered my prayers. Show me all the times when I've cried out for you, and how you delivered me, or spared me, or blessed me. I know you have always been with me. I repent for any time in my life that I have overlooked what you've done for me or how you've answered my prayers. Today, help me to see you clearly. I ask you, God, to fill me with wisdom and knowledge of you and your Word. Lead and guide me in my comings and goings. I pray these things in confidence, by faith, knowing that you hear me and I will always overcome. In Jesus' name, amen.

Darkness Flees
When I Have Faith

BIBLICAL TRUTH

> "You are the light of the world. A city that is set on a
> hill cannot be hidden. Nor do they light a lamp and
> put it under a basket, but on a lampstand, and it gives
> light to all who are in the house."
>
> Matthew 5:14–15

I want you to imagine for a moment that you are sitting in the crowd listening to these words of Jesus Christ: "You are the light of the world." Wow. For much of my life, I felt like being a Christian was about praying a prayer to go to heaven someday and trying not to sin until I got there. These few words from Jesus reveal that there is a much greater purpose for all of us. We are meant to be lights. And not just personal lights that keep us from being in the dark, but lights that show outward to others. Jesus says we are to give light to everyone around us. This means that wherever we go, if we are walking in the light as He is in the light, darkness has to flee.

This morning when I came in to spend time with the Lord and then type a few pages of this book, I flipped on the light switch and the light came on. There was no epic struggle between the light and the dark; the darkness simply left because the light overwhelmed it. How true this is for a Christian walking in the light as Jesus is in the light. When we live by faith, trusting fully in God and the finished work of the cross of Christ, we have the great privilege of watching darkness flee as we walk in truth. God's Word is even referred to as a light: "Your Word is a lamp to my feet and a light to my path" (Psalm 119:105). Today, we can walk confidently into dark places because we have the Light of the World living inside of us. We have the Holy Spirit working within us, using us as lights to a dark world, and we have the Word of God in our hearts, lighting up any dark areas that need to be transformed by His truth. Today, allow God's Word to penetrate your soul and light up your heart and mind. Then, allow the Holy Spirit to shine through you for all to see. The world might be dark, but you're equipped with light.

PRAYER

God, I thank you today that you love me. What a privilege it is to be loved and to be known by you. Thank you that your Word is truth, and that you desired to put your light inside of me so much that you would send Jesus to the cross. Thank you for paying the penalty for my sin and making me a brand-new creation. Today, I desire to be used by you to light up the darkness in my life. Thank you for not leaving me empty-handed and powerless, but giving me the free gift of salvation and the presence of your Spirit. I am never alone, and I know that I can confidently face any darkness in my life or in the world around me because the Light of the World lives within me. Help me today to understand more and more what it means to shine for you. I don't want to hide my faith under a basket. Help me to not be so concerned with my own life that I am not shining for anyone else. I pray that today, as I go, you would keep me close to you. Help me to remember that there are so many who need you, and all they might need today is someone to shine a light on them. I love you God, and I know that I will always overcome, because darkness is overcome by light every single time. I pray this in your name, Jesus, amen.

Day 27

I Can Move God's Heart

BIBLICAL TRUTH

So the LORD relented from the calamity He had threatened to bring on His people.

Exodus 32:14

This interaction between Moses and the Lord is one of the first where we see how love and compassion from humans have the ability to move God's heart. The context here is that God was going to destroy the Israelites, who constantly turned their backs on Him and worshipped false idols. God told Moses to leave Him so He could consume the people and exalt Moses into a great nation. Moses pleaded with the Lord on behalf of his people, but also on behalf of the image of God. Moses didn't want the Egyptians to think God was a harsh God by leading His people out of captivity only to kill them in the wilderness. God was moved by Moses's compassion and did not carry out this threat.

We also see Abraham, in the book of Genesis, contending with God not to destroy Sodom and Gomorrah if he could find a few righteous people in it, although there were none. And we see this in the life of Jesus, who was frequently moved with compassion that led Him to act. We serve an alive God. A God who cares, who has a heart and has shown us that throughout Scripture. How amazing is it to know that we can move God's heart with our lives?

God is watching you and looking upon you, not at the outward appearance, but at your heart. He sees your motives and intentions. Let those motives and intentions be ones that move His heart today. Let the way you intercede for your family, your city, and your nation move the heart of Almighty God. Let the way you love and contend for love in all situations move God. Moses could've easily agreed with God and taken the promotion, leaving the stiff-necked people behind. They were, after all, slowing him down. But Moses chose love over self, and that act moved God's heart and spared a nation. May we do the same.

PRAYER

God, thank you that you're alive. You're not a dead God. I love you and I worship you as my King and my Lord. Today, I ask you to fill me. If there are any areas in my life that are lacking in compassion or love, I ask you to fill those places. I ask you for a revelation of your love today. Show me the heart that Moses had on that mountain, that would move your heart to spare the people. Show me the love for people that would cause Abraham to contend with you. Show me the kind of love that would move Jesus with compassion. I want to move your heart, God, and I know that only by being filled with your love can I do it. Everything that's good inside of me is from you, and I'm asking you for more. I want to honor you and please you with my life. I thank you for loving me and making me a new creation. Thank you for saving me from myself and my sin, and from death. Today, I desire to love you and the people of this world more than I ever have before. I thank you that you're always with me, and I know I will always overcome because you live inside of me. I pray this in the name of Jesus, amen.

Spiritual Gifts Are for Me

BIBLICAL TRUTH

> Earnestly pursue love and eagerly desire spiritual gifts, especially the gift of prophecy.
>
> 1 Corinthians 14:1

I grew up in the church, and for twenty-five years I didn't know about the spiritual gifts. The churches I attended did not talk about them and they certainly did not demonstrate them. What a shame this is. The first miracle I ever saw was not in a church, but in a Nordstrom in Tacoma, Washington, with my best friend, Jacob Coyne. We saw a woman instantly healed of twenty years of painful arthritis in her whole body. I had just gotten born again, and had been reading the book of John and then the book of Acts and was convinced that the gifts of the Spirit didn't "die with the apostles." If this was true, why would Paul, the author of 1 Corinthians, be telling this church in Corinth to eagerly desire the gifts? No, Jesus told His followers that there are signs that followed the *believer*. He said we could ask anything in His name, according to the will of God, and it would be done.

So, what's the will of God? Jesus came and said He only did what the Father was doing, and only said what He was saying. Jesus healed the sick, raised the dead, cast out demons, cleansed lepers, and gave incredible words of knowledge—and then He charged us with doing the same thing, and empowered us to do it by giving us the Holy Spirit. Everything Jesus did was the will of God. It's been made known to us. Wow. What a privilege we have to believe in what Jesus said, and to pursue the life that He lived on this earth.

We, too, can lay hands on the sick and watch them recover by the power of God. We can cast out demons in the name of Jesus Christ. We can pray for resurrection power over the dead in the name of Jesus, and we can prophesy. We are disciples of Jesus just like the people in the Bible were. As you go, remember that the motivation for every spiritual gift is love. This verse in 1 Corinthians 14 comes just after one of the most quoted passages in Scripture, 1 Corinthians 13, where Paul explains what love is. Even in this verse, he first says to earnestly pursue love before desiring the gifts. When you pray, deliver, raise, or prophesy, do it all from a place of love and unto the glory of God. All glory belongs to Him, because it's through Him that all these things are possible.

PRAYER

God, I thank you for loving me. I choose to believe, by faith, that you want to use me to do impossible things on this earth. I believe that you desire to use me to heal the sick, to raise the dead, to deliver the demon oppressed, and to prophesy. I ask you to fill me with your Spirit, even now, to walk in this power. I desire to see the sick healed. I desire to see those oppressed by demons be set free. I desire to see the dead raised to life, just as you did. I desire to prophesy and speak things that reveal the heart of men, that they may know you are God. I desire all of these things because I believe the world will know you are real and that you love them when they witness miracles. Use me to bring heaven to Earth, Lord. I love you and I believe I will always overcome, and see sickness and death overcome by your name. In Jesus' name I pray, amen.

Day 29

I Can Move Mountains

BIBLICAL TRUTH

> "Assuredly, I say to you, if you have faith and do
> not doubt, you will not only do what was done to
> the fig tree, but also if you say to this mountain, 'Be
> removed and be cast into the sea,' it will be done. And
> whatever things you ask in prayer, believing, you will
> receive."
>
> Matthew 21:21–22

I love that this discussion between Jesus and His disciples is in the Bible. It is one of the most empowering passages in the entire book. Jesus gives the disciples the breakdown on what the limitation in this life is when walking with God: nothing. Jesus, in His own words, said that nothing is impossible for us if we have faith. The disciples were marveling over a fig tree that Jesus had cursed a day prior, which had now withered and died. And while they're marveling over a tree, Jesus proceeds to tell them they can do the same thing to mountains. The only thing they must do is believe and not doubt. Jesus spells it out plainly in more verses than just this one, that we have everything at our fingertips because of Him. When we pray in accordance with the will of God, by faith, we will see the impossible happen.

What are some mountains you're facing in life? They might be physical mountains, such as debt or sickness, or they could be intangible things like mental health struggles or relationship issues. Whatever they may be, Jesus has empowered you to speak to them and command them to move. Stand firm on His Word today as you face these mountains and declare who God is in the midst of your circumstances. God desires for you to be free so that you can help others get free as well.

PRAYER

God, I thank you that you love me. You knew me before the foundation of the world, and saw my unformed body as you knit me together in my mother's womb. Your love is so intentional, and I receive it over my life today. I thank you that you desired relationship with me and sent Jesus to Earth to die on a cross so that I could live. Thank you for your sacrifice, Jesus. I thank you that in your name, I can move mountains. I thank you that you have so empowered me to speak to the obstacles in my life, or the lives of those around me, and command them to leave in your name. I believe in you and what you've spoken. Father, I repent for any time that I've ever been intimidated by mountains I've faced. I thank you that you're showing me that I'm not without hope, and that there's no reason to fear or worry. Thank you for shaping me and molding me every day to look more like you, Jesus. Help me today to see the way you see, so that when I encounter a mountain, I'll tell it to move just like you would. I want to be just like you, and I know that I'll always overcome every obstacle I face because you're with me. I love you, and I pray these things in your name, amen.

Day 30

I Can Heal
the Sick

BIBLICAL TRUTH

"And as you go, preach, saying, 'The kingdom of
heaven is at hand.' Heal the sick, cleanse the lepers,
raise the dead, cast out demons."

Matthew 10:7

For the next four days we are going to dive deeper into
this charge from Jesus to the twelve disciples. Jesus is
speaking to them and telling them what they are going to be
doing as they journey to share the gospel. The first thing He
tells them to do is to announce that the Kingdom of heaven
is at hand. Another translation says "is near you." That's
because when we are endowed with the Holy Spirit, we can
see the things of heaven brought to earth. In heaven there is
no sickness, no disease, no death, and no demons. Jesus even
prayed, "Your will be done, on earth as it is in heaven" (Matthew 6:10). When we give people the Kingdom, we have the
great privilege of violently expelling anything within a person that would not be found in the Kingdom, if we believe.

The power to heal, cleanse, raise, and cast out comes from God alone. The access to that power, and the instrument He has chosen to use His power through is us. How wonderful that God would choose us humans as vessels for His power. After telling His disciples to let people know that the Kingdom is there, He first tells them to heal the sick. He doesn't tell them to ask God to heal the sick, but to take authority over that sickness in His name.

When I was a police officer, I didn't have to ask if I was allowed to do my job or to make an arrest. There was a day that I was commissioned by the chief of police as an officer for my city, and it was understood that from that day forward, all authority he had, he was entrusting me with. I did my job in full authority with confidence because I knew my chief had empowered me to do it. Today, as you go, know that you have been empowered with all authority from God. Pray confidently for the sick, knowing that it is not you who is responsible for healing anyone. The power, the healing, comes from the Father, and His operating system is love. You have the great honor of loving those around you, praying in His name, and believing for restoration, so go give the Kingdom to someone.

PRAYER

God, thank you for this day. Thank you for loving me and for choosing me before the world was formed. I believe in you, and that you want to use me to bring your Kingdom to this earth. I accept the commission from Jesus to do what He did, and what the disciples did. I want to be used to see darkness flee. I believe you want to heal the sick through me, Lord. I ask you to give me a heart for the hurting and the broken, that when I see someone in need, I would go love on them. I thank you, God, that when I see someone with a limp, a cast, or a cane, I have an answer. I thank you that I can show them your love and pray for them to be healed, as you did, and believe in you to restore them. I recognize it is not my power, but your power working through me, and all I have to do is believe. Help me to believe today. I want to see the sick healed and made new. I believe that with you, I can see miracles. You are alive, and I know that I will always overcome with you living inside of me. In Jesus' name, amen.

I Can Cast Out Demons

BIBLICAL TRUTH

"Then the seventy returned with joy, saying, 'Lord, even the demons are subject to us in Your name.'"

Luke 10:17

This topic is one that for some reason is controversial in many churches today. It is as if we are of the belief that demons stopped bothering people, or that we don't have any authority over them. Whatever the case is, it seems like we don't hear talk of demons very much from the pulpit. If we don't talk about them or if we pretend they don't exist, we certainly won't have any authority over them or understand what to do when we encounter them. Jesus made it very simple: He told us to cast them out.

The power is in the name of Jesus, and in this truth the seventy who Jesus sent out were rejoicing. That same power is at work today. Don't let anyone tell you that the power of the name of Jesus has subsided, or been removed from the earth, or cannot deliver someone of demonic oppression. I challenge anyone saying that to find one verse where Jesus said that the power would stop after all the biblical characters died, or after a certain period of time. No, Jesus instructed His disciples to go out and make more disciples, reaching the ends of the earth, teaching them to obey everything they learned from Him. You are a disciple of Jesus, equipped to do the work of His ministry by the power of His Spirit.

If you encounter someone who is deep into addiction, weighed down by abnormal anxiety or depression, or is suicidal, you may likely be dealing with some form of demonic oppression. Ask that person if you can pray for them, and take authority over any evil or tormenting spirits that may be troubling them, and command them to leave in the name of Jesus. Ask God to come and fill that person by His Holy Spirit, and begin to speak truth and declare who they are. This truth uproots and replaces the lies, and is a critical piece of deliverance. I have several teachings on this on my YouTube channel, and would recommend learning how to deliver someone from demons. Today, know that you have the authority and ability to do so by the power of the Holy Spirit within you.

PRAYER

Father, I thank you for today. I thank you that you love me and have filled me with your Spirit. I believe what you've said, and that you want to use me and work through me to cast out demons. I thank you, Lord, that your power is still at work today, living within me. I want to be used by you to set free those around me who are oppressed. You said that we would cast out demons in your name, just as you did. Teach me, lead me, and guide me to be able to discern when to pray for someone to be delivered. I love you, God, and I thank you that I will help others overcome their oppression in your name. Thank you for making your home inside of me, and I know that I will always overcome in my own life because you are with me. In Jesus' name, amen.

Day 32

I Can Raise the Dead

BIBLICAL TRUTH

> But if the Spirit of Him who raised Jesus from the
> dead dwells in you, He who raised Christ from the
> dead will also give life to your mortal bodies through
> His Spirit who dwells in you.
>
> Romans 8:11

I covered this earlier in this devotional, but it's never
enough to hear what the verse above is telling us. You
have the *same* Spirit that rose Jesus from the dead. The
power of resurrection was in the Spirit, and now that same
Spirit lives in you. You have living, life-giving resurrection
power inside of you by the person of the Holy Spirit. That
is amazing! Now, maybe you've never heard of someone
raising another person from the dead in your lifetime, but
that doesn't mean it doesn't happen. Talk to enough mis-
sionaries to foreign countries, such as Africa, and you will
hear firsthand accounts of those who have seen the dead
raised back to life through the power of prayer.

Many people I have heard talk negatively about the gifts of the Spirit have never even prayed for the sick or the dead. It really boils down to this: If we indeed have the same Spirit in us that raised Jesus from the dead, does that same Spirit possess the same power, or did the power of the Spirit leave and it was just never mentioned in the Bible? Why would Jesus tell us to go raise the dead if it wasn't possible? Wouldn't it be a sick, twisted joke to set His children up for failure by telling them to go do something they never could? God isn't like that. He is a good Father, and His Kingdom and Spirit are just as alive today as they were in the days of Jesus on the earth.

God told us to do it and then empowered us for it. We have the great privilege of believing God and taking Him at His Word. Whether physical death, or the death of a situation, relationship, or something else intangible, know that you have the power to speak life, and see what was once dead come back to life. The resurrecting power of Jesus Christ is active and working within you. If you encounter something that is dead or dying, speak to it and command it to return to life in the mighty name of Jesus Christ.

PRAYER

> God, thanks for loving me today. I love you and I believe you are who you say you are. I believe your Word is alive, sharp, and active. I believe that what you've said in the past is just as true today as it was then. I believe that you desire to use me to raise the dead, whether physically raising a person from the dead or raising a dead situation to life. I ask you to

fill me with your boldness and confidence, that I may speak to these dead and dying situations and call them as though they were not. I ask you to fill me with your Spirit to go out and call dry bones to live again. God, I desire to be fully consumed by you to the point where I don't care what anyone else says. I lay down my disbelief today and ask you to help me. Help me believe what my flesh may struggle to grasp. Help me to look at a dead situation and see the potential for life. Help me to see with your Spirit and not with my flesh. I want to see the way you see so that I can do what you did. You are my Father and I am your child, and I want to be just like you. Thank you for making me your own. I know I will always overcome with you. In Jesus' name, amen.

I Can Preach the Gospel

BIBLICAL TRUTH

And He said to them, "Go into all the world and preach the gospel to every creature."

Mark 16:15

Have you ever wanted to talk about Jesus with someone but you weren't sure if you were capable? Maybe you felt like you'd be better off sending them a YouTube video or a sermon you heard, because you just weren't qualified. While there's nothing wrong with sending someone a good teaching, you need to know that Jesus wants to use you and your mouth to share His gospel. In the verse above, Jesus is sending out His disciples. But as we covered in the previous days, these commissions weren't just for them. He told them to make more disciples, who would make more disciples, and so on. Today, we find ourselves disciples of the man who said these words, and our charge is the same that it was to the Twelve who walked with Him.

Go out into all the earth and preach the good news of Jesus Christ. You have been given permission by Jesus Himself to carry out the Great Commission. Go tell the world of the redeeming power of the blood of Jesus, who set us free from sin and death. Go tell the world that all of this was done because of the love of God who wanted you to have a relationship with Him. Go tell the world your testimony, and how the gospel set you free, something you never could've done on your own. Go tell the world that the same power that set you free can set them free as well. This is the gospel, that Jesus loved us so much that He chose the cross, He chose death, so that we could live. We can't get to God on our own because of our sin, so Jesus paid the price as the perfect sacrifice, and His blood washes away all our sin. Now, we can pursue a relationship with God through Jesus Christ. What an honor. Once you are saved by Him and receive the revelation of what you were truly saved from, you can't help but share. Sure, there's always someone out there who can "share better than I can," but God wants to use your voice too. Will you let Him?

PRAYER

God, thank you for loving me and for saving me. Thank you for sending your only Son to Earth to pay the price for me to be forgiven and to find my life. Thank you for making me a new creation. Thank you for washing me clean and putting your love and your Spirit inside of me. Thank you for giving me a new life. Today, I give you my doubts and my fears. I choose to believe that you want to use me to share the gospel. I repent for ever speaking something over myself that you weren't saying. I repent for ever believing a lie about myself that you don't want me to spread the gospel, or that I'm not qualified, or that you'd rather use someone else. I believe your Word that says it's for everyone. I believe your Word that says I'm qualified because you say I am, by the blood of Jesus. I surrender my doubts and my fears to you, and I ask you to use me to boldly proclaim your truth. I believe I am holy and blameless and righteous in your sight because of the blood. I believe I am right with you and that my sins have been washed away. Fill me with your Spirit so that I can declare your gospel to the world, just as Peter did when he was filled with the Spirit. I love you, and I know I'll always overcome my fears because you are with me. In Jesus' name, amen.

Day 34

I Can Prophesy

BIBLICAL TRUTH

Therefore, brethren, desire earnestly to prophesy.

1 Corinthians 14:39

Here Paul talks about the gifts of the Spirit and how we should eagerly desire them, but he gives exception to prophesying, declaring that it is the best gift to pursue. He says that when we prophesy to believers and unbelievers alike, the secrets of a person's heart are laid bare, and they know that God is real and among them. Have you ever been in the presence of a prophetic word, or received one yourself? Maybe you've even given words to others. When you experience the power of God revealed through prophesy, it leaves you in awe. I remember praying for someone once as a young believer and having random thoughts pop into my head. One time I specifically remember praying for a friend and I thought of the name "Julie" and then had a follow-up thought, "June 16." I asked the friend if this meant anything to them and they said it was their mother's name and the day of her anniversary. I ended up calling the mother and praying over her, and prophesying what the Lord was speaking to me by His Spirit. At the end of the conversation, she felt incredibly comforted and seen by God, and told me that every word I gave her was accurate.

I've had other times when I believed the Lord was speaking to me and I was incorrect. The beautiful thing of growing in a relationship with God is that He is a good Father and doesn't condemn us for "missing it." God wants us to trust in Him and grow in the gifts He has given us through His Spirit. Maybe you feel like the gifts aren't for you, or you "tried" and it didn't "work." Just like anything else in life, quitting in your growing in the gifts won't help you get any closer to operating in them. Keep going. Keep taking risks. Today, know that you can be used in every spiritual gift, because the Giver of those gifts desires to use you. Seek first His Kingdom, not His gifts, and He will add unto you everything that is needed to accomplish His purposes. Know that the power and ability to prophesy lives within you, in the person of the Holy Spirit.

PRAYER

God, thank you for loving me today. Thank you that your mercy woke me up today and gave me another chance to shine for you. I pray that your love would be so seen through my life that others have to ask me about it. Today, I ask that you would use me to prophesy. I believe in your Word and that this gift is for me. I ask you to help teach me and guide me to learn how to give words to other people. Use me to reveal to the lost what you are saying about them, that the secrets of their heart would be revealed for the purpose of revealing yourself to them. Use me to encourage fellow believers with words of knowledge and prophecies about their lives. I desire to say only what you're saying, and I believe you will speak to me through your Spirit. I repent of any time in my life that I've disqualified myself from this or any of the other spiritual gifts. I surrender my mouth to you and ask you to use me fully in this area. Thank you for making me yours, and I know that I'll always overcome any obstacle with you. In Jesus' name, amen.

Day 35

I Can Forgive

BIBLICAL TRUTH

"If you forgive the sins of any, they are forgiven them; if you retain the sins of any, they are retained."

John 20:23

This is a major statement from Jesus to His disciples. Earlier in the Bible, we see the Pharisees outraged because Jesus told the lame man that his sins were forgiven. They questioned, "Who is this man who claims to have the power to forgive sin?" Now we have Jesus telling His disciples that they, too, have the ability to forgive sin. I am not sure if we have grasped how incredible it is that we have the gift of forgiveness that we get to extend to others. Sometimes forgiveness can seem like a chore or something hard to do, but what if we actually viewed it as a gift?

Imagine a world where we didn't have the ability to forgive. We'd all be walking around full of offense and bitterness, holding grudges, and putting up walls. Jesus gave us the ability to get free from all those things by forgiving those who need it. My friend Jacob Coyne tells this amazing testimony of the power of forgiveness. Once he was praying for this woman who came forward and asked to be healed. Her hands were completely crippled and stuck in a somewhat clenched position, as if she was grabbing something. After praying and rebuking and casting out, nothing happened. Jacob then heard the Lord speak about her family. When he asked her about them, the woman became irate and said she hated them because of a situation that had taken place and never got resolved. Jacob told her about the power of forgiveness, as well as the power of holding onto unforgiveness. As he did, the woman began to repent, and declared that she forgave her family. After this prayer, both looked down and saw that the woman's hands had been totally healed.

Today, know that forgiveness doesn't have to feel good to your flesh for you to do it. You might feel very real pain toward someone, or a group of people, and not understand how to even begin to forgive them. Know that this act of forgiveness is done in faith and has nothing to do with how you feel. Release those who have hurt you from your bitterness or resentment, and declare today that with the help of God, you will forgive. You can do this.

PRAYER

Father, I thank you today that you love me and have forgiven me. I was your enemy because of my sinful nature, and you still loved me and showed that love by sending Jesus to the cross. Jesus, I thank you for your blood that was shed and your body that was beaten and bruised in order to purchase my redemption and my forgiveness. I believe your Word, which says I have the ability to forgive those who hurt me. Jesus, you were able to forgive those who crucified you as you hung on the cross. Help me to have that kind of love inside of me that holds no record of wrongs. I choose by faith to forgive those who have wronged me. Whether these things were done on purpose or in ignorance, I will forgive because you forgave me when I didn't deserve it. Thank you for loving me and for shaping and molding me to look more like you. I will always overcome because you live inside of me. In your name, amen.

Day 36

I Can Overcome Temptation

BIBLICAL TRUTH

No temptation has overtaken you except such as is common to man; but God is faithful, who will not allow you to be tempted beyond what you are able, but with the temptation will also make the way of escape, that you may be able to bear it.

1 Corinthians 10:13

This verse has within it the power to set you completely free from the concept that you're "always going to sin." This verse says that as a Christian, you don't have to. I'm not preaching perfectionism or saying that I never sin. What I am saying is exactly what the Bible is saying. Because of Christ, we have been set free from sin. We aren't slaves to it anymore. This view is important because we will never live free if we don't even believe we can be.

Paul states that what you're facing in the realm of temptation is common, not unique or specific to you, and that there is *always* a way out by leaning on Christ. Often in temptation, young people will come to me and say that they feel overwhelmed and that they didn't have any other choice. While I believe it felt that way, that statement reveals that we rely on our feelings too much. You may feel like there's no possible escape from the situation you're in, but the Word of God says otherwise. We live by the Spirit of God, not our flesh, and have been set free from sin by the power of the blood of Jesus.

Whenever you begin to feel temptation creeping in, run to Jesus. Flee from temptation and seek the Father in prayer. Memorize this verse and recite it over yourself when you are feeling weak. Ask God to help reveal to you if you're responsible for some of your temptation. Maybe you're putting yourself in compromising situations that are prone to bring temptation about. Maybe you're being a little too careless with your scrolling on social media or streaming services such as Netflix or Hulu. Ask God to help keep you from temptation to sin, and be diligent to obey His voice when He speaks to you to get out of a situation. Today, know that it is possible to overcome temptation by leaning on Jesus Christ. You've been set free, and sin is no longer your master. Pursue righteousness!

PRAYER

God, thank you for loving me today. I thank you for setting me free from sin and its power over my life. I worship and praise you today that you have made me a new creation. I am no longer a slave to sin, but a slave to righteousness. Help me to believe every-thing your Word says about me. I choose to believe, by faith, that I can always overcome temptation by leaning on you. I never want to make excuses for my sin, and I repent for any time that I have. I thank you, God, that you don't condemn me, but love me and are calling me to a higher place of purity in my walk with you. Show me any areas that I am opening myself up to temptation, so that I can give them to you. Help me to always flee from temptation. I hate sin! My desire is to honor you and serve you with my life. I know I can always overcome temptation with you living in me. I pray this in Jesus' name, amen.

Day 37

I Can Break Off Curses

BIBLICAL TRUTH

"Assuredly, I say to you, whatever you bind on earth will be bound in heaven, and whatever you loose on earth will be loosed in heaven."

Matthew 18:18

Death and life are in the power of the tongue.

Proverbs 18:21

Here, again, Jesus is talking to His disciples and revealing to them the depth of their authority. They have the power to heal the sick, raise the dead, cast out demons, cleanse lepers, forgive others, and now bind and loose. To bind means to tie or to constrain. To loose means to release or set free. Jesus is explaining that, in this spiritual war, we have authority. Proverbs also tells us how much power is in the tongue. What we say has power, and it can either bless or curse someone.

As Christians walking in relationship with God through His Holy Spirit, we have all authority on earth to break off curses. Sometimes people throw their words around loosely and don't understand the long-term effects they can have on people. Look at victims of verbal or emotional abuse, or those who were bullied harshly in school. Often, they share about their struggles with identity, self-worth, and other areas of life that have been negatively impacted by the words of other people. Words matter, and as a Christian we have the Word which brings life. Today, know that you have the power to break generations of curses off those around you by speaking life. The blood of Jesus has broken the curse of sin, because Jesus became that curse for us on the cross. Now, we can bind any demonic curses that have been performed or spoken over a person's life, and loose or release the Kingdom over them. Where the enemy once occupied space in their lives, or even your life, you can speak the truth and watch the power of God break off all evil. Even by completing this devotional, you might be breaking off lies and word curses that have been spoken over you, or that you may have spoken over yourself. Choose to speak life today. The power of a tongue speaking life in the name of Jesus is enough to uproot all evil.

PRAYER

God, thank you for loving me before I was ever formed. You saw me and knew me before the foundation of the world, and you said my life was so worth living that you would send your Son to die on a cross. Thank you for paying the price to redeem my life and set me free from sin and death. I receive your life, Jesus, in exchange for mine. I believe that within the tongue is the power of life and death, and I want to be a person that always speaks life.

Help me to only say what you're saying. Help me to have self-control in the area of my speech and to honor you with my words. Help me to break curses and death off those around me, by speaking love in your name. I speak life over myself and come out of agreement with any curses that have been spoken over my own life. I can do all things through you, Jesus, and I know that I will always overcome in your name, amen.

I Can
Tear Down Lies

BIBLICAL TRUTH

> For the weapons of our warfare are not carnal but
> mighty in God for pulling down strongholds, casting
> down arguments and every high thing that exalts itself
> against the knowledge of God, bringing every thought
> into captivity to the obedience of Christ.
>
> 2 Corinthians 10:4–5

We are in a war. And Paul states here that it is not
a carnal one—not one that is flesh against flesh,
but spiritual. Did you know that you are in a spiritual
war? We know because of the Word of God how this
war ends: Satan and his army will be defeated and put
to shame, and tossed into the lake of fire for all eternity.
Until that day, we have the great privilege of taking up
our swords and standing firm in the army of the Lord.
Paul tells us that our weapons aren't physical swords or
shields, but thoughts and words. The enemy often tries
to place strongholds over us, convincing arguments and

high things that are contrary to the Word of God. We are instructed to pull down the strongholds, cast down the arguments and high things, and take every thought captive and make it obedient to Christ.

Have you ever had a weird, evil, or perverse thought come across your mind for no reason at all? Some people begin to condemn themselves for these thoughts, thinking, *I'm a Christian. Why am I thinking this? Aren't I born again? Do I need deliverance?* I'm here to tell you that not every thought that comes across the screen of your mind belongs to you. The enemy is always trying to speak to us, discourage us, and present arguments that are against God. The enemy is always suggesting sin to us, tempting us, and trying to get us to live by our flesh. Paul tells us that we have the ability to defeat these weapons of the enemy's warfare. The next time you get a weird thought, tear it down and take it captive by saying something like this in prayer: "Father, I thank you that this is not my thought. I want nothing to do with this. I am holy, righteous, and blameless because of your Son and what He did on the cross. Thank you for making me knew and making me hate these thoughts. My heart is so pure because of you. I love you, Lord."

A simple prayer like that, every single time you get a weird thought, will disarm the enemy. How long do you think he's going to keep plaguing you if every time he does, you run to the Lord? Keep fighting the good fight of faith, and know that you are not helpless to bad dreams or intrusive thoughts. Make an effort to replace those lies with truth, and make those thoughts obedient to Christ as soon as they come to your mind. You will overcome.

PRAYER

Father, thanks for loving me. Thank you that because of Jesus, I am holy, righteous, and blameless in your sight. Thank you for making me new, for putting your light and your love inside of me, and for calling me your own. Today I know that you want to use me to shine for you. I thank you for empowering me to take every thought from the enemy captive. I will not take ownership of a thought that isn't mine. I know I can always overcome bad thoughts with you. I love you. In Jesus' name, amen.

Day 39

I Can Change My Nation

BIBLICAL TRUTH

"Nor do they light a lamp and put it under a basket, but on a lampstand, and it gives light to all who are in the house. Let your light so shine before men, that they may see your good works and glorify your Father in heaven."

Matthew 5:15–16

On Day 16 you declared that you were made to shine, and over the last five weeks you've declared that God wants to use you, but to what extent? Do you believe that God could use you to change an entire nation? Why wouldn't He? After all, the Light of the World lives within you. Do you think this light was only meant to light up your house or your family's house? No. Jesus said that you are a city on a hill, providing light for all to see. You are not a light that is meant to be hidden, but elevated and put on a lampstand, burning brightly and showing those around you the way.

Think about a lighthouse, standing in the midst of winds and rain, storms and all kinds of weather, but continuing to shine. The lighthouse is a guide, a beacon of hope to those ships out at sea. You are like a lighthouse. You will face storms, trials, and tribulations just like everyone else, but what if it is possible to guide others during these times? What if it is possible for you to shine in the midst of the trials of life? What you will find is that when you do, people will look to you as a source of hope. People will see Jesus in you the most when you have every right to complain but choose not to. People will see that Christ lives in you when you're joyful when anyone else in your situation would be whining or groaning.

If you want to change your nation, you must first start with yourself. Make sure that no one, including yourself, has the ability or is given the right to put a basket over your head. Shine for Christ in every situation, and watch how your light is elevated onto a lampstand. In order to see your city, state, or nation become a light, you must show them how to shine. Today, you are going to ask God to help you shine for Him regardless of what you are facing or will face. Then you will ask Him to use you to change your nation. If God can use David, a young shepherd boy, or Paul, once a murderer of Christians, to change a nation, He can use you too.

PRAYER

God, thank you for loving me today. Thank you for shaping me and molding me to look more like you every day. I honor you and worship you as the Lord, as my Savior and my King. Thank you for saving me.

I was so lost without you, heading to hell and stuck in sin, and you made me brand new. Thank you that you have called me the light of the world. You have put your light inside of me, God, because you desire to shine through me. Today, I give myself to you. I ask you to help me shine in all situations. I die to myself today, and crucify my flesh that would want to groan or complain. I want to think about others, not only myself. I believe that you can use me to change my nation. I ask you to open doors for me to be able to speak into the people of my city, my state, and my nation. Fill me with your boldness, that I may see your glory revealed in government. I know you haven't given up on my country, and I believe I will always overcome with you in me. In Jesus' name, amen.

I Can Make Disciples

BIBLICAL TRUTH

"Go therefore and make disciples of all the nations, baptizing them in the name of the Father and of the Son and of the Holy Spirit, teaching them to observe all things that I have commanded you."

Matthew 28:19–20

"Go therefore…" What a charge! We've been given permission. We've been empowered with the authority from Jesus, and He's now encouraging us as we run this race with endurance. In life, it can be easy to get caught up in what we are doing and forget about what He asked us to do. This doesn't mean that every single one of us has to quit our job, sell our home, and move into a mud hut in Africa as a missionary to make disciples. Let's look at where God has you right now. Are you telling people about Jesus at your job? What about at your school? Are you allowing God to work through you, to shine as a light to those around you? This could be a good moment of reflection, with no judgment whatsoever.

Look at your own life and examine yourself honestly. Do you hide your faith in God and your relationship with Him under a basket when you're around certain people, or are you shining brightly for Him? Do people you interact with on a regular basis know that you're a Christian, or would it be a surprise if you came right out and told them? Know today that God's desire is to reveal Himself to you and through you. You've been commissioned to go. Whether at work, at school, while out running errands, or even with family, let the light of Christ shine through you.

You will see that over time, people will begin asking you about the hope that's inside of you. This is a great opportunity for you to be intentional with them. Ask them out for a coffee or a lunch, and tell them about what Jesus has done in your life. Maybe it becomes something you do once a month, or even once a week. Maybe the lunch with one friend turns into two or three friends. Before you know it, you're discipling a small group of people regularly, and helping them grow closer to Jesus. This is what we were made for. Go be a light today. God is with you.

PRAYER

God, I thank you for loving me. Thank you for putting your Spirit inside of me. Thank you for making me into a new creation and saving me from who I used to be, and who I would be without you. I want to be used by you to reach those around me who don't know you or want to know you more. I ask that you would open doors of discipleship for me to begin to pour into others. I ask for wisdom and maturity, that I would be able to lead others to Christ and help them grow in their relationship with you. I believe that I am qualified to make disciples because you told me to do it. I believe I will always overcome any anxiety or doubt I have because you're with me. In the mighty name of Jesus I pray, amen.

My Intercession Is Warfare

BIBLICAL TRUTH

> Therefore I exhort first of all that supplications,
> prayers, intercessions, and giving of thanks be made
> for all men.
>
> 1 Timothy 2:1

Did you know that intercession is for everyone? Sometimes when we hear the word *intercessor*, we imagine some strange older woman in the back room of the church praying violently in tongues. While this might be true in some churches, and some people may have a burden or a gift of intercession, we actually are all called to intercede. Intercession is simply praying to God on behalf of someone else. You can intercede for your family, your friends, your coworkers or your school, your neighborhood, your city, and your nation. I regularly include intercession in my prayer time with the Lord. Your intercession is warfare because you have the ability to contend for things in spirit for those who may be ignorant to the things of God, or in a place of warfare themselves.

The Bible says there is power when we come together in agreement. Have you ever been in need of prayer, and reached out to someone else to stand in agreement with you, and saw breakthrough soon after? There is something that happens in the Spirit when other believers come alongside you in faith.

Today, know that your prayers of intercession matter greatly. In your time with God, don't forget to lift up others and contend for the mountains in their life to be moved. Lift up your neighborhood and believe for it to be free from crime, to be blessed by God, and to be a light to the rest of the city. Lift up your workplace, that your coworkers would be saved and know the love of God. Pray for your family and friends who may be walking through trials, that they would overcome and shine through the process. Go and intercede and watch what the Lord will do.

PRAYER

God, I thank you for loving me. Thank you for empowering me with your Holy Spirit, to live the Christian life just like Jesus did. I pray that you would help me to become more like Him every day. Shape and mold me into the image of your Son, Lord. I submit myself to you and your leadership. I ask you to provoke me in my prayer life to intercede. Speak to me, Lord. I want to pray for things that are on your heart. I believe that my intercession is powerful because it is you working through me. Even now, I lift up my friends and family to you. I pray that they would all know you in an intimate and personal way.

I lift up those in my sphere of influence, whether in person or on social media. I pray, God, that you would deliver them of any oppression they may be facing. I pray that your hand would guide them, and that your love would be known in their lives. Thank you for working through me and using me to shift things in the spirit through my prayers. I love you and I know that I will always overcome with you. In Jesus' name, amen.

I Can Overcome the Enemy

BIBLICAL TRUTH

"And they overcame him by the blood of the Lamb and by the word of their testimony, and they did not love their lives to the death."

Revelation 12:11

This verse is a strategy from heaven. Revelation is an entire book devoted to the end times, which John saw through a vision. Basically, this verse is a key from the future, telling us what it will take to overcome in the present. First, we need the blood of Jesus, which He has already shed for us. Next, we must defeat the enemy by sharing our testimony of what God has done in us. We cannot be silent, because our testimonies bring breakthrough to the world around us, and remind us of what God did for us. Last, we cannot love our own lives to the point of death. What does this look like when it's lived out in a practical way? It looks like denying ourselves, our desires, our will, and surrendering everything to God.

Think about Peter, who denied Christ three times on the night He was betrayed. How could Peter, one of Jesus' closest disciples, deny Him in what would seem to be His greatest hour of need? It's because Peter was more concerned about His life than Jesus in that moment. Peter knew that if he confessed to knowing and following Jesus, he might end up arrested and beaten, or even killed. Peter loved his own life so much in that moment that he denied his Savior. But there is good news. Peter, later filled with the Holy Spirit, declared the resurrection of Jesus to the same people who killed Him. He denied himself, and in doing so, he overcame the enemy. The enemy exists to silence you, to rob you of your faith and get you to deny Christ and stop following God.

Today, know that you can overcome because Jesus defeated Satan on the cross. To see this victory and to put the enemy to shame, die to yourself and follow Jesus no matter what comes your way. Don't make the same mistake Peter did, who denied Christ but then regretted it and wept bitterly. Follow Jesus, even if it means losing your life. Jesus laid His life down for us; we can lay ours down for Him.

PRAYER

God, thank you for loving me today. Thank you that you sent your only Son to die for me so that I could know you. I thank you that right now, you're with me and I am with you. Thank you that you live inside of me and are making me more like you every day. Thank you, God, that because of you, I can always overcome the enemy. You have defeated him and placed him under your feet, and today I can live from a place of victory. Thank you, Jesus, for going to the cross, defeating sin and death and the grave, and purchasing my right to become a child of God. I repent for any time that I've ever been afraid or given too much credit to the enemy. God, you are so much greater, so much stronger, so much bigger than any devil I could ever face. I thank you that you've never been defeated, and that because you live inside of me, I'll never be ashamed by the enemy. Life may seem difficult at times, but nothing is unseen by you, and you're always working on my behalf. Help me grow in faith. Today, I rest in the promise that you'll never leave me or forsake me, and that I will always overcome in the name of Jesus. Amen.

WEEKS 7–9

ACTIVATION

Day 43

I Will Be a Doer of the Word

BIBLICAL TRUTH

"But everyone who hears these sayings of Mine, and does not do them, will be like a foolish man who built his house on the sand."

Matthew 7:26

But be doers of the word, and not hearers only, deceiving yourselves. For if anyone is a hearer of the word and not a doer, he is like a man observing his natural face in a mirror; for he observes himself, goes away, and immediately forgets what kind of man he was.

James 1:22–23

We live in a world that says a lot of things but doesn't necessarily do them. I think of a "campaign promise" in politics. A campaign promise is something a candidate will say they are going to do in order to get you to like them and vote for them. When the time comes after they've won the election, it seems that those promises never make it into the actual administration. If you've ever voted for someone or elected someone for a team at work or in school, and they didn't carry out what they said they would, you feel pretty disappointed and maybe even deceived. There are even those that say they'll do one thing, and then do the complete opposite.

Jesus said, in regard to His teachings, that we must be doers of the Word and not fools who only hear. James reinforces that, comparing someone who doesn't as one who forgets their own reflection. I want us to examine ourselves today before the Lord. Remember that God is merciful and gracious, and that His kindness leads us to repent. He's not sitting in heaven waiting to crush us, but to deliver us and help us along the narrow path. With this in mind, ask yourself, "Have I made any 'campaign promises' to God?" Are there any things you've told God you would do, or that He's told you to do, that you never followed up on? Did you ever ask God to get you out of a tough situation, promising Him something on the back end if He did, and now that you're free, you still haven't held up your end? Have you read the Bible or heard good sermons that convicted you to make a change, but you never did?

I want to encourage you today to know that the grace of God is ready to empower you to do those things. Don't take the path of the fool who hears God's Word but never does anything. Don't believe the lie from the enemy that says you can give God or other people lip service but never follow through and put those empty promises into action. Choose to make a change, right now, to be a person who does what you say you're going to do, and who does what God tells you.

PRAYER

God, thank you for loving me today. Thank you
that you weren't just a God of words but of action.
Today, I'm asking you to help me always be someone who is reliable. I want you to be able to count
on me when you speak to me, whether by your
Spirit or through your Word. I want to be trusted by
you to do what you've said. God, help me to follow
through with others in my life. I want to be known
as someone who does what they say they will do. I
repent for any empty promises I've made, and I ask
you to help me live with conviction and integrity,
and to be a person of my word. I know I'll always
overcome in your name, amen.

Day 44

I Will Lay Hands on the Sick

BIBLICAL TRUTH

> "And these signs will accompany those who believe…
> they will lay their hands on the sick, and they will be
> made well."
>
> Mark 16:17–18

I remember when I first read this verse as a new believer. I got so fired up because I knew that Jesus wasn't just speaking to a select group of people but the body of Christ as a whole. He didn't say, "These signs follow the elect." Or, "These signs follow those with a ministry degree." No. He said that the signs would follow the *believer*. That is you and me. We have the great privilege of believing in what God has said in His Word, and according to this verse, one of the signs that we actually believe is that we will lay our hands on the sick.

Earlier in the Gospels, in the book of Matthew, we were charged with healing the sick in the name of Jesus. I love this passage in Mark because it makes it even easier for us. It simply says to lay our hands on the sick. How often are we doing this? Especially in this period of history we are in, nearly two years into a "global pandemic," we have people who are afraid to get within six feet of each other, let alone lay their hands on them. What if we actually walked in a place of faith where we didn't live our lives afraid of sickness? What if my world view was about others being healed, and not about myself getting sick? The coronavirus has made the majority of the world self-conscious and experts in the art of isolation and social distancing. It has instilled fear into so many, void of statistical data, facts, or real science.

I don't know how you feel about that topic, but in my community and in my house, we still hold onto the Word of God more than the update of the day from the news or the White House press conference. We still believe that God is a healer, and Jesus said that a sign that you actually believe He heals is that you'll go lay hands on the sick.

Between 2020 and 2021, I saw more miracles and supernatural healings than I did in the previous five years. God doesn't stop for a "pandemic." You have the great honor of displaying faith and giving people the Kingdom in a time when fear and sickness is gripping them. Today, if you are in a place of faith to do so, lay your hands on those who need to be healed, and pray for them to be restored in the name of Jesus. Whether they have a cast, a cane, or a cough, God wants to use you to lay your hands on them, so that His power can work through you.

PRAYER

God, thank you for loving me today. Thank you that today I have access to you through the Holy Spirit. I am so thankful for our relationship, and for how you bring peace to my heart and my mind. I believe in you and in your Word, and today I surrender any fear or doubt about your ability to heal or to use me to do it. I want to be a person of faith. I want to lay my hands on the sick and watch them recover so that you can receive the glory. I want to see sickness banished in the name of Jesus. Help me to bring hope and healing in this dark time. Help me show the world that you are real, and that fear is a lie. I love you, and I know I will always overcome fear and sickness because you are with me. I pray this in Jesus' mighty name, amen.

Day 45

I Will Be Generous

BIBLICAL TRUTH

And when Jesus was in Bethany at the house of Simon the leper, a woman came to Him having an alabaster flask of very costly fragrant oil, and she poured it on His head as He sat at the table. But when His disciples saw it, they were indignant, saying, "Why this waste? For this fragrant oil might have been sold for much and given to the poor."

But when Jesus was aware of it, He said to them, "Why do you trouble the woman? For she has done a good work for Me."

Matthew 26:6–10

When you are captivated by Jesus, you see the world differently than those who aren't. This woman, who on earth will forever be unnamed, will always be known for her act of generosity and selflessness toward our Savior. This woman was captivated by Jesus, and her love for Him and recognition of His worth led her to pour out an extremely expensive perfume onto His feet. The disciples didn't even have a grid for this kind of offering, and were thinking about the money it could've produced. I'm so thankful for the disciples, because it shows me that you can literally be walking with Jesus Christ in the flesh and still miss it sometimes. Let's learn from them here and see how they were corrected by Jesus.

This woman saw Jesus and was overtaken by love for Him. She recognized His worth and gave her best to Him as a response. Jesus had not even died for their sins yet, but even still she knew He was worth it all. My friend, today you must know that giving Jesus our everything is the least we can do. He has paid it all for us and redeemed us from our sin nature. He has poured out His blood for us and saved us from the penalty of sin which is a spiritual death and eternal separation from Him. May we be generous in giving our time, efforts, and resources back to Him as a thank-you.

Jesus also told the disciples that when we give to the poor or the needy, we are giving to Him. Today, let compassion and gratitude lead you. May you be consumed with the generosity of Jesus, to humble Himself and come to earth and do what He did. Ask God today if there are areas of your life that He wants to grow you in, with regard to generosity. Are you making the most of your time, or do you have excess that could be contributed somewhere to help further the Kingdom and change lives? Do you have excess finances? Are there any areas that God is calling you to sow into by faith? Do you have skills or other intangible resources that could benefit the body of Christ? Ask God today if He has any desires for you that you haven't realized yet. Let that same love that Jesus had that led Him to choose the cross compel you to be generous in all you do. After the prayer, you are going to ask God to speak to you. Get quiet and listen for His voice.

PRAYER

God, thank you for loving me today. Thank you for pouring out everything you had to purchase my life. I'm so thankful for how you've changed my life, and I lay it down as a living sacrifice today. Help me to follow you and hear your voice. I'm asking you to speak to me about generosity. Lord, are there any areas of my life that you've called me to give back to you, that I'm not already doing? I am listening for you to speak to me now, and I know I'll always overcome with you. In Jesus' name, amen.

Day 46

I Will Pray
for Those in Need

BIBLICAL TRUTH

And pray for one another, that you may be healed.
The effective, fervent prayer of a righteous man avails
much.

James 5:16

When I was newly born again, I began having a desire
to do something that I'd never done before: pray for
people. Now I don't just mean telling a family member, "I'll
pray for you," but actually praying right when the request
was made or the need was seen. I would see someone with a
cast and want to pray for them right then. I would hear that
someone was sick and pray for them on the spot. I would
be talking to a friend on the phone and hear a need for
prayer about a financial or relational issue, and ask them if I
could pray over the phone.

There is something powerful that happens when we step
out in faith and pray. I have noticed my faith grow more
and more as I stepped out and prayed for someone in

person. I've also noticed a big response in those that I pray for. Many people are touched at the thought that you would take the time to agree with them in prayer right there. I've actually had people tell me that they had never had someone come lay hands on them and pray with them outside of a church setting, and even a few people say they never saw it in church. Let's make praying in public for others a normal thing. Instead of just telling someone you'll pray for them later, take thirty seconds and pray for them right then. Watch how God reveals Himself in that situation and see His power displaying through the act of two or more believers coming into agreement.

PRAYER

God, thank you for loving me today. I believe in you, and I believe in your Word. I love you God, and I choose to live by faith today. I tell my flesh to be quiet, because I'm living by the Spirit regardless of what I face. I thank you, Lord, for the gift of prayer. Thank you that I have the ability to commune with you through prayer. I was once a sinner and cut off from you, but now, because of the work of Jesus, I have total access to you and I am no longer a sinner but a saint. I declare that I will begin to pray for those in need. I believe that my prayers are powerful and that you hear every single one. Help me today to encourage others in prayer. Help me to have faith to believe for your will to be done when I pray. I'm asking that you would give me your heart for the needy and the poor in spirit. Help me to see the way you see. Help me to give them the Kingdom when I see them. I thank you for working in me and through me by the power of your Holy Spirit. I yield myself to you and your guidance today, and I know that I will always overcome because you live in me. I pray this in Jesus' name, amen.

Day 47

I Will Take Risks

BIBLICAL TRUTH

> Thus also faith by itself, if it does not have works,
> is dead.
>
> James 2:17

I have seen this verse used in so many ways to justify so many beliefs, but there is one clear message that we cannot miss: true faith requires action. Imagine me sitting in a chair and God speaking to me about writing this book. I could sit there day in and day out, saying, "God is going to use me to write a book. I've never written a book, and I'm not sure how I'll do it, but God told me He wants me to." Now imagine me still sitting there to this day talking about what God spoke to me. You wouldn't have this book in your hands if I had not put my faith into action. My taking the steps to actually write this and publish it show that I trust God enough to do what He's asked me.

Here's another example. Imagine being in the jungle on an exploration and coming to a suspended foot bridge high in the air, with the Amazon River below. Can you picture it? It's about three feet wide and one hundred feet long, and it shakes if the wind blows. The thin and worn slats of wood that are held up by old strands of rope don't bring much comfort to you, but you boldly declare, "I will cross this bridge. I can do this." James 2:17 says that if you don't cross that bridge, your faith is dead and just talk. If you really believe that you can do it, then you will put your faith into action and do it. Now this could seem like an extreme, unique scenario, but the principle is the same. True faith will compel you to act. As I type this, I'm picturing you saying a prayer as you confidently cross, leaning on the comfort of the Holy Spirit to calm your nerves. For some of you, this adventurous scenario is right up your alley and you're running across. Whoever you are and whatever scenario you find yourself in, let's be people who trust in the Lord, and prove our trust by letting our faith in Him drive us to action.

Don't condemn yourself if your faith isn't where you hope it to be yet, because the Bible says we are all at different places in our walk with God. What God wants is a willing heart. Are you willing to surrender your fears and your doubts to the Lord, and do the things He's called you to? Just like the bridge, it might seem difficult or even impossible, but that's where true faith shines. Lean on God for the impossible today, and remember that faith is actually spelled R-I-S-K.

PRAYER

God, thank you for loving me today. I thank you for the gift of faith. Thank you that it is possible to trust in you, and that I'm not alone. God, I don't know where I'd be without you. I don't know where I'd be if I didn't have you to lean on when life seems impossible. Today, I ask you to fill me with the revelation that you're always with me. I believe it because you said it, but I'm asking you to help me see that truth in a way I never have before. I want to take risks for you, Lord. I want to do things in faith that I could never do without you. I trust you and I know that you're always with me. I know that I'll always overcome because you live in me. I love you, and I pray this in your name, Jesus, amen.

Day 48

I Will Surrender to God

BIBLICAL TRUTH

I have been crucified with Christ; it is no longer I who live, but Christ lives in me; and the life which I now live in the flesh I live by faith in the Son of God, who loved me and gave Himself for me.

Galatians 2:20

Surrender was always a bad word when I was coming up in the military as a young lieutenant. Surrender meant you lost. Surrender was unacceptable. As a Christian, surrender is the answer. Paul goes as far as saying he's not even living anymore, but Christ is living through him. I know that for twenty-five years of my life, as someone who grew up in the church and declared Christ but didn't live for Him, this was not how I lived. I lived a life that was all about me, with Jesus incorporated into it. My life existed to serve myself, and I would invite God to join me by praying that He would make things happen for me. This verse above is the true Christian life, and is a response to the great love from God that would send Jesus to the cross for us. When Jesus died, so did I. When Jesus was crucified, so was my flesh. When Jesus was raised from the dead, I was also raised from the old, sinful man, into a brand-new creation. I now live as a vessel for Christ to work through. My life exists to give a body to the will of God through His Son, Jesus.

Full surrender is laying down my will, my desires, and my goals and asking God what His will, desires, and goals for me are. Full surrender is asking God to wear me like a glove. A glove doesn't dictate anything the hand does or even have any input. The glove is fully surrendered to the will of the hand. Asking God to use you in this way is saying, "God, use every part of me and every part of my life for your glory. I submit to you fully." Today, allow God to work in and through you by fully surrendering to Him. Do you believe that He can accomplish His will through your life? Give it to Him and watch what He does. Does God like your job, or does He have a new one for you? Does God like where you're living? Does God like the friends who you hang out with? The answer to all of these could be yes. But examine yourself. When is the last time you asked God about your life?

I went twenty-five years without even thinking about asking God what *He* wanted, and just did what I wanted and prayed it would all work out. I believe there's a better way, and I believe that the one I call my Lord should be given plenty of opportunity to speak into my life and tell me what He would like for me. If I call Him my Lord, then I must submit to Him as Lord. After the prayer, give God some space and time to speak to you about any areas in your life that He may want to use.

PRAYER

God, thank you for loving me today. Thank you for putting your Spirit inside of me. I know that I'll never be alone a day in my life because you're with me. I want to fully surrender to you so that I can be used by you however you want. Reveal to me if there are any areas of my life that you desire to use or change. I don't want a life where you're incorporated. I want you to be my life. I'm asking you to speak to me now, I'm listening, and I know that I'll always overcome because you're with me. In Jesus' name, amen.

Day 49

I Will Tell Someone About Jesus

BIBLICAL TRUTH

The woman then left her waterpot, went her way into the city, and said to the men, "Come, see a Man who told me all things that I ever did. Could this be the Christ?"

John 4:28–29

A Samaritan woman came to get water and ended up having a life-changing conversation with Jesus. I won't summarize the story, but it's only twenty-nine verses in John 4, and I encourage you to read it, but the main point of this exchange is that Christ was revealed to this woman. Because of the laws and culture of the day, this woman and Jesus should have had no business talking to each other. However, because of the encounter and the revelation of Christ that she experienced, verse 28 says that she left her waterpot and went back to the city. She left the very thing that she had come for.

This is no small deal, like leaving a glass of water on the counter and going back to the couch. This woman would put in work every day to get her pot to the well, draw it, and carry it all the way back to her home. She did not have running water to bathe or cook with, or fresh water to drink, so she would come draw at the well. What would compel her to leave in either such a rush or so distracted that she would leave her pot and go home waterless? She couldn't help but talk about Jesus. She defied the culture. She spoke to the men and spoke up in the city and began telling everyone who would listen to come see Jesus for themselves.

Can I encourage you with a simple truth today? Telling someone else about Jesus doesn't happen out of religious obligation. When I began preaching on the streets and in stores, it wasn't because I became endowed with some Christian superpower. It was because I had been alone with Jesus on my bed, when no one else was looking, and I began to know Him. I knew who I was before I met Him, and who He made me to be, and my response was over-whelming thankfulness. I couldn't help but tell others about Jesus because what He had done in my life was so powerful. Just like this woman who had an encounter with Jesus and left everything in her hands to run and tell, would we have the same zeal and desire? Her moments with Jesus overcame any possible anxiety or fear of speaking in public or break-ing culture.

Today, let your time with Jesus consume you, and fill your heart to the point of overflow. You, too, can tell the world about Jesus. Make a declaration to yourself today that you are going to tell one person about Him. Whether at the store, at work, at school, or while out for a walk, stop and tell someone that God really loves them and that's why He sent Jesus to the cross. If they stick around to talk, ask them if they know God, and have a conversation. You'll be amazed what happens when you go in faith.

PRAYER

Father, thank you for loving me. Thank you that I am holy, righteous, and blameless in your sight because of Jesus. Thank you for making me new. Thank you for saving me from sin and death. Today, help me to share about you to someone else. I want the world to know you, and I know I can overcome any anxiety or fear with you, in Jesus' name, amen.

Day 50

I Will Fast

BIBLICAL TRUTH

> "Moreover, when you fast, do not be like the hypocrites, with a sad countenance."
>
> Matthew 6:16

> As they ministered to the Lord and fasted, the Holy Spirit said, "Now separate to Me Barnabas and Saul for the work to which I have called them."
>
> Acts 13:2

> Do not deprive one another except with consent for a time, that you may give yourselves to fasting and prayer.
>
> 1 Corinthians 7:5

Fasting is one of those topics that didn't seem widely talked about in most churches I was a part of growing up. At most, the church would observe a forty-day fast during Lent and encourage giving up things like soda, chocolate, or social media. While doing these things can absolutely be great to break bad habits and give more attention to the Lord, the purpose of fasting was so much greater than trying to stay off your phone for a little longer each day for six weeks. A true biblical fast is to go without food (not without water). Biblical fasting is believing on the Lord to sustain you as you deprive your flesh of what it craves. Jesus said things like "when you fast," the book of Acts talks about the disciples praying and fasting, and Paul's letter to the church at Corinth instructed that fasting and prayer were the only reasons that a married couple should abstain from physical intimacy. It is implied and taught throughout the Bible, from Jesus Himself to the disciples, that fasting is a normal part of the Christian life.

If you are looking for a fresh fire with regard to fasting, please go on Amazon after today's devotional and order The Atomic Power of Prayer and Fasting by Franklin Hall. That book changed my life and my view on fasting, as well as on extended fasting. It's a short read, is less than $10, and its value is priceless. I can truly say that my eyes have been opened in the area of fasting and I'll never be the same after reading it. Whether you decide to pick up a copy of that book or not, know this: The Christian life involves fasting, and it is something we must do in order to suppress our flesh and give room for our spirit to hear and see God clearly.

Fasting and prayer is the equation to revelation. You must do both. Just fasting without prayer does not achieve the same results. We do not fast and pray to "move God"; we do so to move ourselves and our noisy flesh out of the way so that we can catch a vision for our lives or our situations. Don't just fast when you "feel led," because it probably will never happen. Make fasting a routine part of your life and watch what God does with your discipline and obedience.

PRAYER

Father, thank you for loving me. Thank you for loving me even when I was a sinner, hostile in my mind and in my nature toward you. Thank you for redeeming me by the blood of your Son, Jesus. God, I desire to see you more clearly and know you more. I will make fasting a part of my life, not out of religious obligation but because I see the value in it. Thank you for the gift of fasting, and I know that I will always overcome every trial and obstacle because of you. I pray in your name, Jesus, amen.

Day 51

I Will Make Time for God

BIBLICAL TRUTH

"But you, when you pray, go into your room, and
when you have shut your door, pray to your Father
who is in the secret place; and your Father who sees in
secret will reward you openly."

Matthew 6:6

Do you spend time with God? I don't mean just listening to a sermon or worship in the car or at the gym, or
praying while you're at work. All of those things are great,
and I do them as well. What I'm asking is, is there a specific
time that you set aside when it's just you and the Lord? Is
there time in your day set aside that no one else, no other
thing, has access to? A time when your phone can't bug
you or distract you, when you're not doing other tasks, but
simply sitting in the Lord's presence? I have noticed that
since I've been born again, there is a direct impact on my
life from making time just for God, as opposed to when
I don't or when I miss for a few days. I still feel "off" if I

don't get my alone time with Him, and the same goes for my wife. I love that we can always commune with God no matter where we are, but Jesus makes a clear statement here by telling the disciples that they aren't just going to be in their rooms, but to shut the door.

Why do we shut doors? Privacy. Intimacy. Things we don't want to broadcast to the rest of the home, or things that we don't want interrupted. Jesus calls this "the secret place." Do you have a secret place? Do you have a place where you go sit with God in total intimacy? Mine is in my office, and every day, early in the morning, I get up and spend a few hours with Him. No one else has the ability to contact me during that time, unless it's an emergency, and I won't schedule anything during it either. I do everything I can to protect it, and my wife does the same with hers. If you don't, I'd highly encourage you to heed the advice of Jesus and do so. Imagine this: I'm married and my wife desires to hang out with me, but I only spend time with her in the car, or while doing errands, or around other people. Imagine that whenever we are at home, just the two of us, I'm always doing something else. Imagine her asking me to come spend time with her, just us, and I bring my phone with me. Do you think we would have a lot of intimacy? Do you think we would have deep conversations? Do you think she would feel honored, heard, or valued? Or would she feel like she has to share me with my phone or the rest of the world?

Our relationship with Jesus is more real than even our earthly relationships. He died so that we could have intimacy with the Father, through Him. Let's seek Him today in the secret place.

PRAYER

Father, thank you for loving me. Thank you that you sent your Son to this earth to pay the price for my sins, so that I could know you. Thank you for making me brand new and removing all of my sin. Thank you for calling me holy and righteous, and seeing me as blameless before you. Today, I worship and praise you. I want to spend more time with you, Lord. Help me as I try to remove the clutter and distraction from my life, so that I can seek you. I will set aside time to be with you, because you are worthy of it all. Thank you for desiring to meet with me. I know I will always overcome in you. In Jesus' name, amen.

Day 52

I Will Face and Overcome My Fears

BIBLICAL TRUTH

> The Lord is my light and my salvation; Whom shall I fear? The Lord is the strength of my life; of whom shall I be afraid?
>
> Psalm 27:1

Fear is something that many people deal with on a consistent basis. Whether it is fear of something tangible, such as spiders or darkness or poverty, or something intangible such as social anxiety or insecurity, fear is real. But in this psalm, David brings a revelation to the light that has the ability to change us, if we allow it.

The Lord is our salvation and our light in the darkness. Have you ever stopped to think about the fact that our eternity as Christians is completely secure in Christ? Jesus said in John 3:16 that as Christians, we are never going to die; we will simply pass from this earth into the Kingdom with Him. Most fear has to do with being hurt or losing our lives. Other fear has to do with not being accepted, or being rejected. In Christ, neither of those can hold us any longer. Death has been defeated by Jesus on the cross, and now we live with Him. Full surrender to God looks like dying to yourself, realizing that this life is not our final destination, and that there is more for us on the other side of eternity. Truth can uproot much fear, such as knowing that God has accepted you and you need not fear rejection by any man. What man can reject what God has accepted? If you are rejected by the world, you are in good company, because so was Jesus Christ.

As a Christian, you have the ability through the blood of Jesus to be free from the opinions of this world, because God, the Creator of all things, has given you His opinion. Jesus proved His love for you by choosing the cross. When this revelation hits your heart, you get free. When you're free, you don't care what anyone says about you because their opinion cannot compare to God's. You can walk out of your home free from the cares of what people think about you, because your life is hidden with Christ in God (Colossians 3:3) and because your value and worth come from the Father, not the world. You can face your fears of death because death cannot hold you or defeat you, because it is Christ living in you who will never die. With Christ, you can overcome all things. Fear keeps you bound. Today, let's face what we might be afraid to even mention, and know that with Christ, we'll always overcome. He will never leave you or forsake you. You are an overcomer, and you'll always overcome. After the prayer, take a few moments and ask God to reveal any areas of fear, and submit them to Him.

PRAYER

God, thank you for loving me. Thank you that in you, there is no fear. You aren't afraid of anything, and you live within me. Help me today to see you clearly, and to live with my eyes on you. I know that if my eyes are fixed on you, I won't be overwhelmed by what's right in front of me. God, I declare that I trust you, and I know that you have not given me a spirit of fear. You've never left me or failed me, and I know I'll always overcome with you. In Jesus' name, amen.

I Will
Get Connected

BIBLICAL TRUTH

> And let us consider one another in order to stir up
> love and good works, not forsaking the assembling
> of ourselves together, as is the manner of some, but
> exhorting one another, and so much the more as you
> see the Day approaching.
>
> Hebrews 10:24–25

think it's safe to say that the last two years have revealed not only the need to assemble, but the power that comes from it. The 2020 pandemic forced a lot of pastors to make decisions about closing or staying open, amid the tyrannical decisions of local government that put pressure on churches to stop gathering, or stop worshipping out loud, or reduce the amount of people that could gather. Thankfully, in many states, the courts have overturned these decisions by state and local government, ruling that churches should not be limited in any way. In Texas and Florida, among other states, it is now illegal to attempt to restrict or ban the gathering of a congregation.

The root of why we gather is found in the verse above, and it is far greater than a statement made to our city, state, or nation. The writer of Hebrews states the purpose of these gatherings is to stir each other up, to encourage one another because the Day of Christ is approaching. Sadly, just as the verse above states, during the pandemic it became all too easy for people to stop attending church, or to get plugged back in once things began to return to a state of "normalcy."

Has that been the case for you? I want to encourage you today to make the effort to get plugged back into a local church body. You cannot do church online, as much as we would like to think that will suffice. It can be effective for a season, or for those who are physically unable to gather. But online church is by no means a replacement for gathering in person. This verse above refers to a literal gathering, an assembling, of physical people in person. We need to be gathering with like-minded believers and encouraging each other in the faith. If you are a faithful online attender but do not go to a physical church, I urge you to get involved somewhere. Maybe you do attend, but you are not really connected into the body. Volunteer! Join a small group. We were made to commune with God and with others. Take that next step and get involved on a deeper level, and watch your faith and your heart grow as you connect with other people. Don't do life alone. Get yourself surrounded with healthy community, and be intentional about meeting with them regularly. It isn't healthy to run this race alone. The Bible says iron sharpens iron, but it can't sharpen itself. Get around some iron and get sharpened.

PRAYER

God, thank you for loving me. Thank you that you are enough for me. You've purified me by your blood. You said that it is not good for man to be alone, and you gave us the ability to populate the earth so that we could do life together, all for your glory. I ask that you help open new doors for me to connect with others. I repent of any anxiety or fear that I may have had about gathering, and I know that you will help me overcome. I want to be connected with the body of Christ. Help me to make new friends and get sharper in my faith. I love you, God, and I thank you for always hearing me when I pray. In Jesus' name, amen.

I Will Love the "Hard to Love"

BIBLICAL TRUTH

> "Then the righteous will answer Him, 'Lord, when did we see You hungry and feed You, or thirsty and give You something to drink? When did we see You a stranger and take You in, or naked and clothe You? When did we see You sick or in prison and visit You?' And the King will reply, 'Truly I tell you, whatever you did for one of the least of these brothers of Mine, you did for Me.'"
>
> Matthew 25:37–40

When you hear about people who are "hard to love," whom do you think of? I remember growing up in church hearing about people groups that supposedly fit this qualification. There were the homeless, the broken, the needy, the rebels, the prodigals, and others. However, when I think about Jesus, it's hard for me to imagine Him calling any of us hard to love. I can't imagine those words coming out of His mouth.

The truth is that when we call someone hard to love, what we are actually saying is that they don't live or respond the way we are comfortable with, and that makes it difficult for us to continue loving them. I can't find that anywhere in my Bible. We are called to love our neighbor, regardless of how they live or act or respond to us. The passage above is Jesus telling His disciples something incredible that should provoke all of us to be intentional with those in the world who are overlooked.

Jesus says when you care for the hurting and broken, the outcast and the downtrodden, you're caring for Him. That sounds like an invitation to choose love. If we categorize people as hard to love, we will have excuses about why it's okay that we can't love them. What if we truly died to ourselves, and it didn't matter how people treated us, or responded to our efforts, or how they spoke about us? What if we could love with no strings attached? What if we could love on people with no expectation?

Thank God that Jesus didn't put expectations on us. He died for us while we were still sinners. While we were hostile enemies of God, Jesus came and paid for our sin to be forgiven. While we were knee deep in sin and heading to hell, He loved us and never changed His mind about us. May we become that very love as well. There may be people, even close family, in your life who you would've said this about before reading this today. I'd invite you to look through the lens of Christ and reassess how you are loving them. Whether you're in close community with someone, or loving someone from afar with healthy boundaries, make sure there's not an expectation on that person. Even if you know you'll be mocked or ridiculed or talked about, choose to love anyway. God never gave up on you, so don't give up on someone else.

PRAYER

God, thank you for loving me. Thank you for never changing your mind about me. I am who I am today by your grace, and because of your love. I walk in that newness today, and I thank you for making me into a new creation by the blood of your Son. Thank you for justifying me in your sight because of Jesus' sacrifice. You loved me when I didn't deserve it, and I'm asking you to help me love those who might not feel deserving of love. Help me to see everyone as worthy of what you paid for, and to love with no expectations. I know I will always overcome with you, Jesus. I pray in your name, amen.

Day 56

I Will Be
a Good Friend

BIBLICAL TRUTH

"Greater love has no one than this, than to lay down one's life for his friends."

John 15:13

This verse is amazing because Jesus would go on to lay His life down for us, demonstrating the great love with which He loves us, and the love of God that would send Him to earth to pay the price for our sins. Laying down your life requires action and sacrifice; it costs you something. Jesus was not a man of talk but of power.

I chose this verse for today's reading because being a good friend involves intentionality. Being a good friend is going to require some sacrifice. I want you to see the standard for what Jesus said is the greatest form of love: to lay down your life for your friends. Who are some people that come to mind when you think about your close friends? As we do in all areas through this book, I invite you to examine yourself with regard to the kind of friend you are. Do this without fear of condemnation, shame, or guilt. Maybe after examination, you'll see that you haven't been the best friend you could be. If so, let love overwhelm you to change. Maybe you've been an incredible friend. Keep going.

Wherever you fall on the scale of great to not so great, know that Jesus showed us what a good friend does for another. This could be something small like taking one out for coffee or for brunch. Maybe the next time you get asked to help someone move, you make it a priority and work your schedule out so that you can be there to help. I will tell you as someone who has moved many times in the last decade that you really find out who your friends are when you need help moving. Take some time out of your week or month and reach out to good friends who you might not see often and encourage them, pour into them, ask them how they're doing and how you can pray with them. People are precious to God, which is why He paid such a high price. Our careers are great, our hobbies are wonderful, our possessions can be blessings, but people are the only things you can take with you to heaven.

Make today the day that you decide to be more intentional with those in your life who you truly care about. A lifelong friendship is hard to find, so don't take it for granted. If you want something to grow, you'll have to sacrifice your time and energy to feed and water it. Reach out to someone after the prayer today and let them know you're thankful for them, and try to find time to get together. Life is short. Let's be intentional.

PRAYER

God, thank you for loving me. Thank you for showing me what real love looks like, by laying down your life for me. I am so blessed to be loved by you. Thank you for making me new and calling me your child. I am redeemed by your blood and have been set free from sin. Thank you for living inside of me, and help me die to myself daily. Help me to become more like you so that I can love those around me. I desire to show your love to my friends, and to steward my friendships like you would. Help me to live selflessly and to be intentional about pouring into those I call my friends. Thank you for modeling what true love looks like. I know I'll always overcome with you as my God. I pray this in your name, Jesus, amen.

Day 57

I Will Run Well

BIBLICAL TRUTH

> Therefore we also, since we are surrounded by so
> great a cloud of witnesses, let us lay aside every
> weight, and the sin which so easily ensnares us, and
> let us run with endurance the race that is set before
> us, looking unto Jesus, the author and finisher
> of our faith.
>
> Hebrews 12:1–2

How often have you heard the Christian life described as a race? The writer of Hebrews charges us with running it with endurance. Sometimes I meet Christians who seem like they're barely hanging on, waiting for Jesus to come back and save them from life because it's gotten too hard. Maybe you even find yourself in that place right now. Know that the charge to run well wasn't left without instruction on how to do it. Anyone can point out what's wrong with something, but a good teacher or coach will tell you how to do things better or more proficiently.

The writer here tells us that the way we run with endurance is by looking at Jesus. It is Jesus who gave us the gift of faith by showing us who God was, and giving us the Holy Spirit. Jesus has revealed God to the world, and now we can know Him on an intimate level. This passage says that Jesus is also the finisher of our faith. He will complete what He started. Let this knowledge fuel you to run this race well. Think about the day that we will stand before the Lord and how you want to feel when you look back on your life. I hope to be able to say, "Lord, I ran as hard as I could for you."

We have the honor and the great privilege of laying our lives down for Christ and running as if we were in a physical race. Have you ever been in a race? Maybe in the schoolyard as a kid, or in track or cross country in school. The goal of a race is to crown a winner, and you have the ability to win, A "win" as a Christian is finishing this life strong, full of faith in Jesus, having endured until the end. You might suffer what feel like defeats in your life, but know that the way you win and the way you run well is by keeping your eyes on Jesus and staying in faith. The enemy may come and try to get your eyes on him, or on yourself, but remember who our champion is. Today, know that you *can* run this race well. It's not about having the biggest ministry or giving the most money to the poor, but about faith, and faith that endures till the end. If you've been sitting on the sidelines, it's time to get up, lace your shoes up, and get in the race.

PRAYER

God, thank you for loving me. Thank you that you have put your life and your light inside of me, and today I'm going to shine for you. Thank you for setting me free from the old me, and making me a brand-new creation. Thank you, Jesus, for shedding your blood so that I can live and know God. I look to you today as the fuel for my faith. I look to you, Jesus, as the answer to every situation I'm walking through. I repent for any time I've taken my eyes off you and focused on myself or what the enemy was up to. You, Jesus, are the finisher of my faith. I believe you will finish what you began in me. Help me to keep my eyes on you today so that I can run well. I thank you that my deeds aren't what please you, but my simple faith in you and my obedience to your voice. I know that I'll always overcome and I will finish this race strong with you, Jesus. In your name, amen.

Day 58

I Will Always Overcome

BIBLICAL TRUTH

> For whatever is born of God overcomes the world.
> And this is the victory that has overcome the world—
> our faith. Who is he who overcomes the world, but he
> who believes that Jesus is the Son of God?
>
> 1 John 5:4–5

Here we are on Day 58 and we've arrived at the day that inspired the entire book. "I will always overcome" is a phrase my wife and I have leaned on for the last few years that have brought serious breakthrough in times of testing. Whether financial, physical, or spiritual obstacles, we have always encouraged each other to remember that we will always overcome because Jesus has overcome. This passage says it best: our faith is what overcomes the world. The enemy is after your faith; that's his entire strategy. He can't defeat Jesus, he can't overcome the blood and the cross, but he can try to make you not believe in God. He can do his best to keep you ineffective by messing with your life, because he knows that it will usually send a person spiraling in their mind, shipwrecking their faith. The devil even told God to His face in the book of Job that his entire goal was to get Job to curse God. The devil is up to the same thing today.

How can you overcome? By believing you will because Jesus already has. Whenever my wife, Jessica, and I run into an obstacle, we say, "I will always overcome. I will overcome. I'll always overcome." We say this over and over again until our faith becomes louder than our circumstance. As an act of faith, I've lain on the floor on my face, saying, "I'll always overcome." I'd slowly get up to one knee, whispering it again. Then up to my hands and knees, saying it a little louder. Then eventually rising to my feet, raising my hands above my head and declaring out loud that "I will always overcome!" I would get so filled with faith that tears would fill my and Jessica's eyes, and we would both praise God for the victory that He was going to bring.

The theme of this devotional is to position you to believe you will really overcome. Over the past eight weeks you've said it every single day, and scientifically your brain has been re-wiring itself to believe it. Know that today, you will always overcome the enemy because your faith is in Jesus. Jesus has overcome the world and has called you an overcomer. You may not always feel like one, but thank God we don't live by feelings, but by the Spirit. Say it until you believe it. In Christ, you will always overcome.

PRAYER

God, thank you that I will always overcome. No matter what I'm facing right now, what trials are in my life, what obstacles I have in front of me, I know I'm always going to overcome them. I choose to tell my flesh to shut up, and live by the Spirit today. Thank you, Jesus, for setting me free from my flesh and giving me the right to become a child of God. I thank you that you've enabled me to walk out this life by the power of the Holy Spirit, and to have faith even when life doesn't make sense. I thank you for the peace that guards my heart and mind that surpasses all understanding. I will overcome. I'll always overcome. I worship you and honor you, Lord, as the overcomer, and I thank you for calling me one too. I love you. In Jesus' name, amen.

Day 59

I Will Deny Myself

BIBLICAL TRUTH

> Then Jesus said to His disciples, "If anyone desires to come after Me, let him deny himself, and take up his cross, and follow Me."
>
> Matthew 16:24

Denial of self is the first thing that Jesus instructs us to do if we want to follow Him. Why? Because, as we discussed earlier in Revelation 12:11, the way we overcome is by the blood of Jesus, the word of our testimony, and not loving our own lives to the point of death, also known as denial of self. The reason that denial of self is so critical is because without it, the blood of Jesus has no effect on our lives.

Let me explain it this way: Jesus paid the price for us to be forgiven of our sins and pursue a relationship with Him, on His terms. There is a narrow path leading through a narrow gate, as Jesus said in Matthew 7. We cannot get to God however we want, and Jesus said in John 14 that if we love Him, we will keep His commands. We cannot say we love God but live our entire lives for ourselves. Self is the first thing that has to get out of the way so that Jesus can take residency in our hearts. Paul says that it's no longer he who lives, but Christ in Him, and how true that still is for us Christians today. Pride and selfishness, self-seeking and self-serving tendencies have to go so that the will of God can be done.

If I live for myself, I actually reject the teachings of Jesus and reject His sacrifice because I am choosing my flesh and my life over His. Jesus told these people that the invitation to follow Him is wide open, but it comes with a cost. Are you willing to pay that cost? Did you know that Jesus died so you could be free from yourself? You can actually be free from sin, from addiction and bad habits and ways of thinking that only bring destruction. You can be free from using other people for your benefit. You can be free in order to love. This freedom can only come by the power of Jesus Christ and by choosing to lay down your life for His. Once your life is laid down, you can effectively carry your cross, which we will talk about tomorrow. Dying to self is something I intentionally do, and say, every day. Make the decision today to die to your way and choose His way instead.

PRAYER

God, thank you for loving me and making me new. Thank you for calling me your own, and for sending Jesus to die for me even while I was a sinner. I receive your love today, and I thank you for this life you've given me. It's my joy to be loved by you. Today, I ask you to help me lay down my desires and my will so that I can accomplish yours. You know my dreams and my goals, but, Lord, I want to know yours for me. I choose to deny myself today so that I can put off the old man and put on the new. Thank you for setting me free from me so that I can know you. Help me to accomplish your will today. Use me, Lord! Just like you overcame sin and death, I know that I will always overcome because you live in me. I pray in Jesus' name, amen.

Day 60

I Will Carry
My Cross Daily

BIBLICAL TRUTH

> Then He said to them all, "If anyone desires to come
> after Me, let him deny himself, and take up his cross
> daily, and follow Me."
>
> Luke 9:23

It's so interesting to me that at this point in Jesus' life, He had not yet gone to the cross or told His followers that this was how He would die. The cross represents Jesus doing the will of the Father above His own. Jesus prayed in the garden that the will of God would be done, and did so with such intensity that He sweat drops of blood. Jesus would carry out the will of God by choosing the cross over His own fleshly desires, and ultimately bring salvation and redemption to humankind. He said all of this before He went to the cross.

Notice that Jesus said to "take up *his* cross," implying that we each have a cross to bear. Carrying your cross means doing the will of God for your life, just as Christ did. If we want to partake of His cup, then we must be willing to lay down our will and yield to the will of the Father. Doing so will bring not just blessing but suffering. Jesus said this, but the reward is eternity with Him totally redeemed from sin and the corruption of the world. Paul said that these sufferings we go through don't even compare to the glory that is going to be revealed. Eternity with the Lord cannot compare to our present trials.

Today, as you pick up your cross and carry it, know that your Father in heaven sees you. You are not alone, but have the same Spirit that Jesus had inside of Him—the very Spirit of the living God. Just as Jesus surrendered His desires, choose to surrender all for God and watch Him carry out His will through you. If life has become all about you and what you can accomplish before you die, I'd re-evaluate what's most important to you. I lived for myself for decades, trying to climb the ladder and make some-thing of myself, all while praying that God would bless me through it. When I got born again, I realized that my life was created by Him, for Him. Now, as best I can every day, I lay my life down in the morning and ask God to use me that day for His purposes and His glory alone. Every life decision I make is made after submitting it to Him. Carrying my cross means submitting my plans and dreams and desires before the feet of Jesus and seeing if it's what He wants for me too. Today, let's heed the words of Jesus and lay down our desires so that we can pick up our crosses and follow Him. He is worthy.

PRAYER

God, thank you for loving me and making me new. Thank you for calling me your own, and for sending Jesus to die for me even while I was a sinner. I receive your love today, and I thank you for this life you've given me. It's my joy to be loved by you. Today, I ask you to help me lay down my desires and my will so that I can accomplish yours. You know my dreams and my goals, but, Lord, I want to know yours for me. I yield everything to you and will carry my cross because you carried yours for me. Just like you overcame sin and death, I know that I will always overcome because you live in me. I pray in your name, amen.

Day 61

I Will Live
by Faith

BIBLICAL TRUTH

> Now faith is the substance of things hoped for, the
> evidence of things not seen.
>
> Hebrews 11:1

I love this verse because it makes faith simple. Let me
break this down even further, to the place where it
makes the most sense to me. Faith is believing in something you can't see, and it is what causes you to have hope.
The Bible says that love hopes all things. For there to be
any hope in your life, there must be faith, because hope is
a positive desire for the future that you haven't seen come
to pass yet. The concept of faith is actually very easy; all
you have to do is believe in what you can't see, regardless
of what you do see.

Say you're believing for God to bring a breakthrough in
an area of your life, maybe finances. Faith is looking your
financial situation in the face, not denying it, and saying,

"I see this issue, but I know who God is, and I know that He will always provide for me." You might not see the manifestation happen yet, but you're speaking the truth of God's character over your circumstance. Some people might get caught up praying emotionally and questioning, which doesn't produce faith but anxiety. Have you ever prayed like this: "Oh, God, where are you? Help me. Can't you see that I'm paycheck to paycheck and now my car needs fixing too? Where are you God?" Many cry out to God from this place, but it only makes you more aware of your problem, with no solution in sight. Here's how to pray and stand in a place of faith: "God, I know that things look really bad right now. I'm paycheck to paycheck and my car just broke down and I'm not even sure how I'll get to work, but I know who you are. You are the God of the breakthrough. You are my provider. My trust, my hope, my peace is not found in a paycheck or a promotion, but in you alone. Thank you for loving me and for caring for me. I know I will overcome this trial because you are with me. I don't care what things look like or how bad they seem; I will never stop trusting in you."

Praying like that releases faith. It causes you to declare truth in the midst of your circumstance, and it positions your heart to believe in God through your trial. Maybe today, as you read this, you're thinking of your own obstacles that stand in your way. Take a few minutes to declare who God is over them. Don't tell God how big your problems are; tell your problems how big your God is.

These last three days, I want you to pray your own prayer. I believe I've shown you the format and style of prayer that

I pray every single day that has changed my life. My hope for this entire devotional is that you not only build faith but have learned how to pray effectively. An effective prayer is one done in faith, that releases hope into your spirit and glorifies God. It's a prayer that reinforces the truth of God's Word, regardless of what life or the enemy brings your way. Pray over yourself and reinforce this truth, that you will always live by faith.

PRAY.

I Will Speak Life

BIBLICAL TRUTH

Death and life are in the power of the tongue.

Proverbs 18:21

It's been rumored that the tongue is the most powerful muscle in the body. While, scientifically, this has been disproven, the proverb above shows us exactly how powerful it is. You have the ability to speak life or death over people and situations. Jesus said that He came to bring life and life more abundantly (John 10:10). The thief (Satan) comes to steal, kill, and destroy. If you were to speak death, which person do you think you're aligned with? How about if you spoke life? It's an easy answer when you see it written down in front of you, but sometimes life can squeeze you so hard that whatever is inside of you comes out before you get a chance to filter it.

Don't believe me? Have you ever been cut off in traffic, or gotten rear ended at a red light, and something came out of your mouth that wasn't very holy? In those type of situations, what's in you is what's coming out, and it's too late to try to remember the last best piece of advice you heard about patience and speaking life. Maybe you've had a tough time raising a child, or had a hard friendship where the other person was constantly making bad decisions, and you chose to speak the opposite of life over them: "You're never going to get this." "You're so stupid." These kinds of comments hold more power than we realize, and the enemy loves when we speak them because it's ammunition to his warfare. What we say matters, and it holds weight in the spiritual world.

Maybe you've spoken this way about yourself before: "I'm such a failure." "I might as well give up." "I don't think anyone would care if I died." These things are completely contrary to the Word of God, and are things that God has never said about you. Did you know that scientists did a study where, every day, a person cursed one plant and spoke life into another? They found that over time, the cursed plant began to wither and die, and the other blossomed beautifully. There is scientific evidence for speaking life into the atmosphere, over people, and over situations. Today, choose to be someone that speaks life. Get alone with God and ask Him to reveal what He is saying about your life and the lives of those around you. Get the perspective of Christ driven so deeply within your heart that when life squeezes you, He's the only thing that can come out.

PRAY.

Day 63

I Will Share My Testimony

BIBLICAL TRUTH

> "And they overcame him by the blood of the Lamb
> and by the word of their testimony, and they did not
> love their lives to the death."
>
> Revelation 12:11

You have a testimony. If you've been born again, you have a story to tell. The Bible says that this is one of the ways we overcome the enemy. One of the biggest ways to shame the devil is by telling people about what God has done for you. You were born in sin, heading to hell and a slave of the devil, and the blood of Jesus set you free. You were stuck in selfish ways, pride, addiction, insecurity, depression and anxiety, and by the power of the name of Jesus Christ you were delivered. You were lost and now you're found. You were blind and now you see. This is your testimony.

When you share this, the enemy is reminded of his crushing defeat on the cross, and God is glorified. Many people feel as though they don't have a testimony to share because they haven't "been through enough." I'm here to tell you that you don't have to have the same testimony as someone else. There are people you will reach that they never could, and there are people they'll reach that you can't; it's the beauty of the body of Christ. We all work together to build the Kingdom of God and destroy hell. But you can't destroy hell if you don't tell someone about what God has done in you. When you tell a person about your story, it creates faith that God will do it in them.

As we conclude this book today and reflect on these last nine weeks, what has God done in you? Has your faith been strengthened? Has your prayer life become more intimate and effective? Have you found a sense of peace and joy as you've declared the Word over yourself? This is a testimony. God is always working in us, and when we open our mouths to tell someone about what He did that we never could've done without Him, He gets all the glory. Today, talk to someone about Jesus and share a little bit of your testimony. Whether at the gym, the store, or even at work, ask someone if you can tell them about how your life has changed. Where you were and where you are now are totally different, and that's all because of the Lord who brought you out of the old and into the new. Don't keep it a secret!

PRAY.

About the Author

Shane Winnings is a military veteran who served in Afghanistan, a former law enforcement officer, and a Spirit-filled evangelist. On May 1, 2021, God spoke to Shane to quit his job where he and his wife were very comfortable, making over $100,000 per year with amazing benefits and seniority, into unpaid missionary work. They now serve with One Voice Student Missions (ovsm.com) as full-time missionaries, dedicated to reaching Gen-Z for Jesus Christ. Shane is also a part of The Jesus Clubs, reaching literally millions of students per week through social media! He and his family make their home outside of Dallas, Texas. You can follow him on TikTok, Instagram, and YouTube @thejesusclubs and @shane.winnings.

Made in the USA
Monee, IL
20 January 2024

52120657R00105